PRAISE FOR *BEAT BY BEAT*

"Todd Klick's brilliance shines through his masterfully conceived and beautifully executed *Beat by Beat*, a must read for screenwriters whether you're a total novice or an Oscar-winner—this book is a case study in smarts. I've never been one to suggest that screenwriting (or acting, or wardrobe, or set design, etc.) can be 'learned' by someone without the 'born gift'—but in the case of *Beat by Beat* I suggest this gift can be, and will be beautifully enhanced. Of equal or greater value, *Beat by Beat* will make your screenplay marketable, bankable, producible—and it won't take long before they are calling you and your work 'genius.'"

—**John Philip Dayton**, CBS executive producer, director, writer; *The Waltons, Eight Is Enough, Matlock, The Ray Bradbury Theatre*

"When intuition and verve stall, and your story stops 'writing itself,' Todd Klick's *Beat by Beat* will be your new best friend."

—**John L. Geiger**, coauthor, *Creativity & Copyright*

"There have been other books that have dissected films before, but none to the detail of Todd Klick's *Beat by Beat*. Discover the amazing intricacy of film(s) one minute at a time."

—**Matthew Terry**, filmmaker, screenwriter, teacher

"Screenwriters . . . *Beat by Beat* is a book you'll find most invaluable in your quest to write the next "Monumental Movie of the Millennium"! This book is your pass to the head of the line."

—**Forris Day Jr.**, reviewer and writer, scaredstiffreviews.com

"*Beat by Beat* takes screenplay story structure down to its smallest elemental level, guiding you on a minute-by-minute journey through what makes some of the most popular films resonate so strongly with filmgoers. Klick delivers a book that's specific enough to get you placing all the right moments in exactly the right places, while also being broad enough to allow your creativity to explore and discover."

—**Tom Farr**, writer, teacher, storyteller (whisperproject.net)

"*Beat by Beat* presents a refreshing new take on the age-old challenge of writing a book that will aid and inspire screenwriters. It is a useful tool for jumpstarting the script-writing process, but can also be applied as a way of double-checking story beats on a script well under way. One of its key strengths is it can be adapted to most any visual narrative medium from feature films, short films, and television episodes to webisodes and beyond."

—**Roy Finch**, assistant professor, Chapman University

"A beat sheet that covers fundamentals and genres. Todd Klick has uncovered what makes great cinematic storytelling. A must for anyone in the business to make their film important and lasting."

—**Dave Watson**, editor, Movies Matter (davesaysmoviesmatter.com)

TODD KLICK

Beat by Beat

A Cheat Sheet for Screenwriters

MICHAEL WIESE PRODUCTIONS

Published by Michael Wiese Productions
12400 Ventura Blvd. #1111
Studio City, CA 91604
(818) 379-8799, (818) 986-3408 (Fax)
mw@mwp.com
www.mwp.com
Manufactured in the United States
of America

Cover design by Johnny Ink. johnnyink.com
Interior design by Debbie Berne
Copyediting by David Wright

This book was set in Minion Pro and Gotham.

Library of Congress Cataloging-in-Publication Data

Klick, Todd, author.
Beat by beat : a cheat sheet for screenwriters / by Todd
    Klick.
Studio City, CA : Michael Wiese Productions, 2016. |
    Includes filmography.
LCCN 2015043174 | ISBN 9781615932467
LCSH: Motion picture authorship—Handbooks, manuals,
    etc.
LCC PN1996 .K618 2016 | DDC 808.2/3—dc23
LC record available at http://lccn.loc.gov/2015043174

To Ray

CONTENTS

"I have an idea for your next book," my publisher, Michael Wiese, said over the phone. We somehow synched our busy schedules and wildly different time zones — he in England, I in Los Angeles. I was deep in the midst of five active writing and filmmaking projects and the thought of adding a sixth to the pile was unappealing. But Michael grabbed my attention by saying the following: "I'd like to do something with your *Something Startling Happens* story beats; something more streamlined; a kind of cheat sheet for screenwriters."

I raised an eyebrow, like Spock does when an idea appeals to him: *Hmm, a cheat sheet for screenwriters . . . fascinating.*

I loved writing this book! It gave me the opportunity to create the kind of visual screenwriting guide I *jonesed* for when I first started penning scripts back in Pennsylvania, but could never find on the shelves. It also gave me the chance to develop a power-packed pictorial aide that summed up what I had learned from studying over (currently) 400 successful films in my quest to better myself as a writer. In short, I got to produce my fantasy screenwriting book: a go-to guide that features all the minute-by-minute storytelling secrets I've utilized (and tips I've learned from pros) to pen a bestselling book, option scripts, and sell numerous writing projects for the stage and screen.

It is my hope that this book helps you do the same.

Todd Klick

This book features a blockbuster movie from each of the top-selling genres: Action, Adventure, Comedy, Drama, Horror, and Thriller. The six movies I chose to represent their genres had to meet three criteria, or what I call "The Holy Trinity": 1) Rated 75% or higher by critics on rotten-tomatoes.com; 2) Rated 80% or higher by audiences on rottentomatoes.com; 3) Earned a minimum worldwide gross of $300 million. In other words, audiences and critics not only loved these movies, but the films also made stacks of cash for their happy producers. Two of these films even grossed over an unbelievable *billion dollars*. These six movies are:

ACTION   ADVENTURE   COMEDY   DRAMA   HORROR   THRILLER

These next sections explain the secret recipe. If you ignore this part and go right into cooking your story, the recipe won't work. Take five minutes to read the next few sections and the minute-by-minute beats will be fully illuminated.

The best way to use *Beat by Beat* depends on what type of writer you are. Are you a Stephen King type, or a John Irving type? King said his writing process is *"like walking through a desert and all at once, poking up through the hardpan, I see the top of a chimney. I know there's a house down there, and I'm pretty sure that I can dig it up if I want."* Without a complete idea of where his story is headed, King starts writing the book, making the discoveries as he plows forward. John Irving, on the other hand, outlines extensively, knowing the fine details of each scene and chapter before he even begins writing his novel.

Whether you are a King or Irving type of writer, or you approach story from a completely different place altogether, you can use *Beat by Beat* as a page-by-page metaphor or checklist whenever you're ready for it, or as an idea booster if you get stuck.

If you're an Irving type of writer, you may want to do your research first, develop your extensive outline, write your first draft, then reference this book toward the end to see if you're addressing each minute-by-minute guideline. Or maybe you want to find your story on your own and write a voluminous 300-page first draft to get it all out of your head. Cool, go do it. That's fantastic. But eventually you may want to visit this book to see if your script addresses the successful minute-by-minute beats that all great films use.

When in need, this book can also assist while developing your overall structure or filling in second act weak spots. Use this book to brainstorm with other writers on how your story should advance or conclude, or to think up fresh ways to surprise the audience that is consistent with the minute beats and genre. You can also use this book to fill the gaps in your existing outlines or treatments.

When it comes to my own process, I hone a 12- to 17-page outline until the story is structurally sound, then when I write the script I reference the beat descriptions as found in *Beat by Beat* as I enter each page.

When I first applied the minute-by-minute beats, *that's* when I attracted my first manager and advanced quickly to the Nicholl Fellowship quarterfinals. Soon after I had to hustle to meet another contest deadline with a new script. I didn't have two months to outline like I usually did, so I decided to jump right in and "bang it out blind." Starting at page one with only a grabber opening in mind, I wrote like Stephen King — discovering the story as I went along. As I approached each script page, I referenced each beat to keep me on track so I didn't waste time. I wrote the script in two weeks (a personal record), and sent it off immediately to the PAGE International Screenwriting Contest where I made the finals. Since then, I've optioned and sold numerous scripts. My latest screenplays, using the beats as my guide, have recently attracted A-list production companies which have worked on numerous blockbuster movies like *Star Wars: The Force Awakens, Super 8,* and *Mission Impossible: Rogue Nation.* I owe all this attention to the minute-by-minute insights revealed in this book.

1. I want to make something clear: The minute-by-minute beats you are about to read are *not* taken from the original screenplays or shooting scripts. They are drawn from far superior material: The final stories you see on the big screen *after* they were filtered through the studios' vigorous distilling process.

2. You need to understand that the terms used in this book (like *Main Hero, Ally, Bad Guy, Enemy, Villain, Sidekick*) are flexible and interchangeable from page to page, *depending on what's happening in the scene.*

Sometimes the enemy becomes the hero for a page (in *The Avengers*, Loki becomes the hero for a scene when he faces the intimidating leader of the Chitauri); or the ally becomes the enemy (in *Gone Girl*, Amy's ex-boyfriend, Desi Collings — who saves her when she loses all her money — becomes her enemy).

Sometimes the ally can be an inanimate object (in *The Avengers,* a computer named Jarvis is Tony Stark's ally, revealing information he needs to know), or the hero's conscience can become the bad guy (in *The Hangover,* Stu's guilt becomes his enemy). You must be flexible with these terms from scene to scene or the beats won't work for you.

I also use words like *explosion, damage, warning,* or *threat.* Most times an "explosion" will be a literal explosion, or the explosion could be more figurative, like an *explosion of emotion* . . . A *warning* can be very dramatic or it can be something said subtly through clenched teeth. The dramatic level of these words can change from page to page, too, or

story to story. But what's important to realize is that *they are there.* These beats should be represented on every page, grand or small, or your screenplay may fall short. The reader or audience subconsciously expects these universal patterns. If you neglect to include them, the audience may feel gypped.

3. Try using the minute-by-minute catch phrases. I spent months paring down the phrases so they are descriptive and precise. The phrases were initially one sentence long, but after using them while wrestling with my own scripts, I found myself paraphrasing: "This is Minute 63, I need an *Ally Attack*." Or, "This is Minute 77, I gotta have *The Rumble*." These fun phrases get to the point of what needs to happen in the script — a tremendous time-saver. Writing partners and I use the catchphrases as shorthand. We even use the phrases while developing stories with clients, with other screenwriters, and during pitch meetings. The phrases work for us, and they'll work for you too.

4. If you're fond of using index cards while developing your story, this is a technique you'll find helpful. After you've outlined your movie, scribble the minute-by-minute catch phrases onto 120 individual index cards, each card representing one minute. Then brainstorm on the card original ways you can demonstrate that minute in your story. For example, jot down as many *Friend or Fist* moments you can think of on card 6 (Minute 6 or Page 6 of your screenplay), or write as many *Whew, That Was Close!* moments as you can on card 15 (Minute 15). This'll help you zero in your creativity and force originality.

"What happens if a film is only 85 minutes long? Do the beats you describe get compressed — sometimes two per page?"

Whether the story stops at Minute 94 (like *The Hangover*), or 104 (like *The Conjuring*) or upwards to 120 and beyond (like *Skyfall, A Beautiful Mind,* and *Gone Girl*), the minute-by-minute (page-by-page) beats remain steadfastly consistent. The beats are like piano keys that are fixed into place. But with those fixed keys you can play an endless variety of original rock and roll, jazz, blues, punk, indie, and orchestral music, whatever you fancy. *The Hangover* and *Skyfall* do the *exact* same minute-by-minute beats up until 94. *The Hangover* ends on Minute 94 but *Skyfall* continues, adhering to the remaining Minute 95 through Minute 120 beats. Therefore, compressing story beats is unnecessary.

"If every good movie sticks to these minute-by-minute beats, then why are some movies longer than others?"

Movie lengths vary for this reason: The number and complexity of characters and subplots change from film to film, requiring different lengths to satisfy each unique story arc. But whether the film has a handful of subplots or just one, the writer must still address each minute-by-minute benchmark mentioned in this book to avoid boring the audience — an audience who inherently expects this underlying story rhythm in all the movies they watch.

"Sometimes movies are more than 120 minutes long. Do the minute-by-minute beats extend beyond the two hours mentioned in your book?"

Yes, but since the majority of movies sold and distributed are under 120 minutes I trimmed the book to accommodate the practical needs of the average working screenwriter and filmmaker.

Do these beats work with different genres?

Yes, which I will demonstrate by using six different genres throughout this book. What's great about these beats is that it doesn't matter if you're writing a thriller, a comedy, horror, drama, action, or adventure, or a combination of two or three genres, the underlining minute-by-minute beats are still represented in all successful movies. It's the ground floor of what all movie stories are built upon.

Is this a formula way of storytelling? Won't a formula stifle my creativity?

The definition of "formula" is: "a conventionalized statement expressing some fundamental principle." Is *Beat by Beat* a fundamental principle? Absolutely *yes*. It's a universal principle that is common in all successful movie-stories. You're welcome to avoid these fundamental principles in your movie storytelling, but don't be surprised if agents, managers, studio execs, or production companies don't return your phone calls or e-mails after you send them your script or independent movie. In addition to looking for a fresh voice in your work, they are subconsciously looking for these universal beats, archetypes, themes, arcs, and conflicts addressed in this book when they're reading your screenplay or viewing your film — it's a primal storytelling *need* fashioned over a hundred years of industry storytelling.

If you're an experimental independent filmmaker who is fiercely against anything that whiffs of a set way of doing things, fine, go do your thing. But don't be shocked when your audience falls asleep during your screenings, or walks out altogether. There's a reason why fundamental principles — like those found in geometry or physics — keep a plane in the air or prevent a bridge from toppling over: they work. So it is with the fundamentals of storytelling.

Will these fundamental principles stifle your creativity? Quite the opposite! Once you know the fundamental beats, they free you to spend your creative time thinking of original ways of telling your story each and every minute! For example, once Picasso mastered the fundamental principles of color and design, it freed him to go in a completely different direction visually than all the other painters who preceded him. But here's the thing: Even though Picasso's cubist creations looked radically different than anything else the gallery audiences had seen up until that point, each of his successful paintings, at their core, still adhered to the basic fundamental principles of color and design. Once he mastered the universal basics and applied them, it freed him to spend all his energy on creating original, and timeless, masterpieces. So it can be with your stories.

Will these beats work for short films?

Whether your film is five minutes long, twenty minutes long, or forty-five minutes long, the minute-by-minute beats apply. You still must satisfy Aristotle's theory that all stories need a beginning, middle, and an end, but underneath the beginning-middle-end, no matter what your story's length, the beats as described in this book remain a universal rhythm for any visual storytelling length.

Can I use these beats when writing television pilots?

Yes, the minute-by-minute beats work whether you're writing a twenty-two-minute comedy pilot, an hour-long crime drama, or a two-hour TV movie. The universal story rhythms of *Beat by Beat* apply whether you're watching a blockbuster on a giant Cineplex screen or a popular series on a tiny home television. All visual stories still need Minute 5's *Jaw Dropper*, Minute 14's *Danger Watch*, or Minute 22's *Truth Declared*, etc.

How about a webisode? Do the *Beat by Beat* patterns work for those?

Yes, whether your webisode is three minutes long or up to ten minutes long, the opening minute-by-minute beats need to be applied — along with Aristotle's beginning-middle-end storytelling theory — to satisfy the audience's inherent rhythms and expectations. During Minutes 1 through 10 the audience will need to experience At*tension!*, *The Build*, *The Ratchet*, *Another Notch*, *Jaw Dropper*, *Friend or Fist*, *Friend or Fist 2*, *Something Startling Happens*, *The Pursuit*, *The Discussion*, etc.

How can a director use *Beat by Beat*?

A director can use the minute-by-minute beats as a checklist while working with a writer, developing storyboards with an artist, or on set while working with the director of photography. A director can also use the phrases in this book as verbal shorthand when discussing a story with a producer, actor, or director of photography.

How can a producer use *Beat by Beat*?

If a producer finds a script he likes, but feels there's something missing in its storytelling, the producer can use *Beat by Beat* to diagnose what's missing. The producer can also refer to this book while working with a director to assure his movie is hitting all the same rhythms that all successful movies are utilizing.

How can an editor use *Beat by Beat*?

An editor can use the beats in this book as a minute-by-minute checklist while trimming down a movie. This guide will be a tremendous benefit and time-saver in finding any movie's story rhythm.

How can an actor use *Beat by Beat*?

Actors are the visual conduit for expressing the all-important minute-by-minute story rhythms to the audience. If an actor fails to touch upon each minute's specific rhythm or benchmark, than the director and audience will feel something is lacking in his performance. An actor who has the beats described here in his arsenal will have a distinct subconscious advantage over actors who don't.

Does *Beat by Beat* work in foreign films too? Don't the cultural differences affect the beats?

The beats described in this book apply to *all* successful films, no matter which country they are developed in. Though some of the themes and political concerns may vary from culture to culture, the story rhythms are universal and are at the foundation of every good movie. Even though the Japanese culture, for example, may be distinctly different from the American, Italian, German, or French cultures, their movie storytelling techniques, at the core, still use the exact same beats.

I don't understand: How can a romantic comedy be the same as a horror movie?

Movies are strikingly similar to architecture. Just as a romantic villa built in a sunflower meadow in Tuscany looks wildly different in appearance than an eerie Transylvania castle once owned by Vlad the Impaler, the architectural principles upon which those uniquely different buildings were designed and constructed are *exactly* the same. So it is with movie stories.

Can I use *Beat by Beat* to write a novel?

Novelists have the luxury of exploring and expanding upon the inner workings of their characters, and the ability to allow page upon page of bountiful description. Despite this literary freedom, however, their main function is to tell a good story. Since *Beat by Beat* lays out the consecutive beats of successful storytelling in movies, the novelist can borrow these beats as a guide or checklist, especially if he or she wishes to eventually develop their novel into a feature-length film.

How do I break down movies minute-by-minute for myself?
First, rent the movie you wish to analyze. Grab a stopwatch and click it on until it reaches 1:00 (1 minute), then stop it there. Okay, begin the movie. Now, *when* you restart your stopwatch is crucial. Don't click on your stopwatch as soon as the credits begin. Start when the *story* begins. How do you know when the story begins? It's where the screenwriter most likely began writing the movie after typing FADE IN. Don't start when the credits are running, unless the credits are shown while the story is unfolding (like in *Raiders of the Lost Ark*). Also be on the lookout for what I call "James Bond credits," meaning credits that appear after the big movie opening. Click your stopwatch off during the James Bond credits and music, unless of course they're part of the story. Use this book as a guide as you stop and start each minute, jotting down your own insights.

Sometimes when I break down movies, as suggested in your book, the movie I'm studying doesn't show your beats. Why is this?
Successful movies adhere strictly to the minute-by-minute beats, as demonstrated over and over in this book. On rare occasions the beats are slightly early or late (usually within five to twenty seconds), but the point is: The beats are there, or in the vicinity. If finding the beats is difficult for you, try reviewing Step 2 in *Four Things You Need to Know Before Reading This Book*, and re-read *How do I break down movies minute-by-minute for myself?* (above) until these concepts become crystal clear in your mind. Just like any skill, you have to master the basics and then practice them until they become second nature.

Can *Beat by Beat* be used for graphic novels?
The beats described in this book would be ideal for the visual medium of graphic novels, especially if the writer pens the story between 70 to 120 pages. In such a case, the minute-by-minute beats could be applied page by page, much like a film script.

Can development executives, managers, or agents use this book?
Although there are many astute agents, managers, and development execs in the business, some still struggle to explain exactly what is wrong with a particular script to their clients. While some executives, managers, and agents demonstrate adequate skill at explaining character arc or the requirements of a three-act structure, they can still find it difficult to troubleshoot those numerous pages between major plot points. That's where this book comes in handy: It explores, in depth, all those in-between pages! For example, if you feel your client's script is lagging during pages 51–59, you can flip to Minutes 51–59 in this book to see exactly what needs to happen during those pages.

During the early 1900s silent movie era, writers typed simple scene headings and action descriptions for directors. Then came along Thomas Ince, founder of Hollywood's first major studio facility, who — for efficiency — decided to add interiors, exteriors, and camera angle descriptions. These screenplays were typewritten with specific margins, giving Ince an idea of how long a movie would be. Therefore, one script page equaled approximately one minute of screen time.

By the mid-50s, the powerful studios switched their focus to marketing and distributing movies, relying more on producers to package and pitch them film ideas. This led to writers creating more "readable" scripts for investors, leaving out technical jargon. This approach evolved the screenplay into the modern format known as the Master Scene Script, which includes scene headings, action, characters, parentheticals, dialogue, and transitions.

You can Google "movie script PDFs" to view examples, or you can buy a computer program which mimics the spacing and type of this popular format. I use Final Draft.

NOTE: *To simplify the reading experience, I usually refer to the Main Hero with masculine pronouns, but the Hero can, of course, be female.*

Here are the classic Jungian archetypes I see most often in successful movies, with one of my own included. They are: **Main Hero, Sidekick, Maiden, Wise Old Man, Villain, Henchman, Shape-shifter, Trickster, Eternal Child,** and **Mother Figure.**

MAIN HERO

There can be many heroes in a movie story, so how do you know which is your Main Hero? The Main Hero experiences the most extreme transformation. In *The Avengers*, Captain America, Tony Stark, Black Widow, Thor, and Bruce Banner all share heroic moments. So who's the Main Hero then? In this particular story, Tony Stark is the Main Hero because he undergoes the most extreme arc: selfishness to self*less*ness. The Main Hero is also the person who, toward the end of the movie, sacrifices his flaw for the good of others — a noble act he suffers for, but is also *rewarded* for. Tony Stark overcomes his flaw of selfishness by undertaking a suicide mission for the good of mankind, but in doing so he experiences pain when he topples violently back to earth. But for doing so, Stark is rewarded with the other Avengers' deep respect.

The Main Hero is also orphaned in some way. Either he's a literal orphan, where one or both parents are dead, or he is emotionally or physically distant from his mother and/or father. Why are orphans so effective in storytelling? Because being an orphan is an instant way to draw sympathy from your audience. Why? Because we've all felt alone in the world at some point in our lives. I felt alone in the world when I drove across the United States by myself to pursue my dreams of writing in Los Angeles, a city where I knew no one. Soon, however, I found Sidekicks, Wise Old Men, Mother Figures, and Maidens to help me navigate my way through all the Shape-shifters, Tricksters, Henchmen, and Villains I would encounter during my quest.

SIDEKICK (ALLY)

The Sidekick (or Ally) is the Main Hero's buddy, pal, or confidant. He (she) is there to lend an ear, advice, support, and to challenge the Main Hero's flaw. He is the Samwise Gamgee to Frodo in *Lord of the Rings*, or Margo to Nick in *Gone Girl*. Using Sidekicks is also a trick screenwriters use to show what the Main Hero is thinking through dialogue, as opposed to novels where we read the character's thoughts. Sidekicks help the screenwriter avoid relying too heavily on narration.

MAIDEN

The Maiden is the Hero's love interest, or the Maiden can be a female who represents innocence, purity, or naiveté.

WISE OLD MAN

The Wise Old Man is someone older than the hero who offers wisdom or guidance: a mentor. He is the Obi-Wan or Yoda to Luke Skywalker, or Dumbledore to Harry Potter, or Mister Miyagi to Daniel in *Karate Kid*. Sometimes Wise Old Man can be a false Wise Old Man, like Lamar Burgess, John Anderton's boss and mentor in *Minority Report*, who turns out to be (Spoiler Alert!) the killer.

VILLAIN

The Villain is the main bad guy, but it's key to understand that the Villain doesn't see himself as the bad guy. He sees himself as the Hero. He is the Main Hero's primary opponent who will draw out, expose, and test the Main Hero's flaw.

HENCHMAN

The Henchman is the Villain's right-hand man. The Henchman is a skilled and formidable foe who stands between the Main Hero and the Villain. The Main Hero must defeat the Henchman to get to the Villain.

SHAPE-SHIFTER

An obvious Shape-shifter is someone like Bruce Banner who physically transforms into the Hulk. But the Shape-shifter is also someone who may seem good at the beginning but reveals himself to be bad, like Carl in *Ghost* who betrays his best friend Sam (Patrick Swayze). Or the Shape-shifter may seem bad, like Old Man Marley in *Home Alone*, but in the end he saves young Kevin's life. The Shape-shifter's loyalties are often unclear; he will often change his personality or allegiance in extreme ways.

TRICKSTER

The Trickster is mischievousness personified. He likes to mock and crack cunning jokes. He's the comic relief whose loyalties can sometimes be in question. He's a smartass. He is Han Solo in *Star Wars*, or the Joker in *Batman*, or Captain Jack Sparrow in *Pirates of the Caribbean*.

	Main Hero	Sidekick	Maiden	Wise Old Man	Villian	Henchman	Shape-Shifter	Trickster	Eternal Child	Mother Figure
Skyfall										
The Avengers		JARVIS								
The Hangover										
A Beautiful Mind										
The Conjuring										
Gone Girl										

ETERNAL CHILD

The Eternal Child can be a literal child, or he can be an adult who is childlike. Forrest Gump is a perfect example, or Frodo or Harry Potter. They represent innocence and provide hope through their childlike wisdom.

MOTHER FIGURE

The Mother Figure is nurturing and caring. She can be temperamental and volatile as well, like M to James Bond, or Galadrial in *Lord of the Rings*.

Most successful movies use a minimum of eight of these archetypes, as seen in the chart on page 19 featuring our case study blockbusters. Some characters can also occupy two archetypes in the same film.

To create great twists in your story, try the unexpected with your archetypes. No one would expect the Wise Old Man to be a serial killer, or the Main Hero's Sidekick, Maiden, or Mother Figure to be a traitor, or the Henchman to betray the Villain. You can create shocking moments by flipping the audience's expectations of the archetypes.

THEME

Theme is what your movie is *really* about. It's the clothesline you hang all your scenes and dialogue on. The best movie for theme in this book is *Skyfall*. The theme is: Old Ways versus the New Ways. The movie explores different shades of this theme: Aging Bond has "lost a step;" Mallory wants aging M to retire; Young Q still "has spots" as Bond points out and can kill people with one computer keystroke; Silva, who's Bond's age, uses new technology to try to rule the world. *Skyfall's* scenes and dialogue are rich with this theme, which adds a depth uncommon in most action movies.

When we finish watching *Skyfall* this thought crosses our minds: *Sometimes the old ways are best.* The audience or readers of your screenplay should always walk away having learned a one-line sentence from your story — a bit of

Q and Bond explore *Skyfall's* theme: Old Ways vs. the New Ways

wisdom, tied to the theme, that makes them better human beings. Even after viewing a movie with a tragic ending, we should learn something positive that makes the experience worthwhile.

In *The Hangover*, Phil allows himself to be bullied — his flaw

HERO'S FLAW

The Flaw is what your Main Hero struggles to overcome throughout the entire movie. He or she is clueless of this flaw at the beginning but an Inciting Incident and an adventure come along that will expose and test this flaw. In a happy ending, the hero overcomes his flaw and is rewarded because of it. In a tragedy, the Main Hero fails to overcome his flaw, but we learn from his mistakes.

A flaw can be selfishness, anger, unforgiveness, hatred, addiction, etc. Examine your own life. What's the flaw that you are unaware you have, or you're in denial about? What's that flaw that's holding you back from being a better human being? What's the flaw that life keeps hammering at and exposing until you finally learn to overcome it? What's that flaw that — if you don't overcome it — people will view as a tragedy when you are dead?

The flaw is tied to the theme. In fact, your whole story is about whether the hero will overcome his flaw or not. Yes, there may be action scenes, thrills, drama, and horror happening all around your hero, but those events in a story happen in order to expose and test the hero's flaw in hopes the experience makes him a better person.

THE PERFECT ARC

The best character arcs are the ones where the Main Hero goes through a 180-degree turnaround. For example: Hate to Love, Selfishness to *Selfless*ness, or Hopelessness to Hope. The more extreme your Main Hero's arc, the better the ride for your audience.

At the beginning of *The Hangover*, Phil allows himself to be bullied by his fiancé Melissa. In the end, however, Phil refuses to be bullied by Melissa and breaks up with her — his 180-degree arc.

PURPOSE OF A SCENE

A scene is one step forward in your hero's trek toward confronting his flaw. A scene reveals something new and significant about your hero or the other archetypes, either through action or dialogue. A scene reflects the theme in some way. A scene shows conflict, opposition, or tension. Most scenes can be anywhere from an eighth-of-a-page to five pages. A good scene doesn't meander or linger: It enters the drama as late as possible and exits as early as possible. A scene that lacks friction or tension, or fails to address the theme in some way, must be cut.

PURPOSE OF DIALOGUE

"When we tell a story in cinema," Hitchcock once advised Francois Truffaut, "we should resort to dialogue only when it's impossible to do otherwise." In other words, after you've exhausted every conceivable way to cleverly *show* conflict and tension in your scene (as if you were writing a silent movie), *then* you may insert dialogue to advance the story.

And in that dialogue you must express what each of the archetypal characters would truthfully say in that particular situation. Their words must sound fresh and original, devoid of clichés. Each of the characters must speak genuinely in accordance to their unique personalities, diverse upbringings, educational backgrounds, regional cadences, ages, IQs, worldviews, and philosophies.

Dialogue must not be "on the nose" (characters saying precisely what they mean) unless absolutely necessary. Your dialogue must utilize the power of subtext instead, meaning: The characters say one thing but think another. A classic example of subtext is in *The Godfather* when Don Corleone tells his godson, Johnny: "We'll make him (the Hollywood producer) an offer he can't refuse." Subtext: *We'll threaten his life.*

4-ACT STRUCTURE

I use a four-act structure simply because the act breaks for the three-act structure always seem clumsy to me: Act 1, Act 2a, Act 2b, Act 3. I'm not a fan of the "a" and "b" thing. The four-act structure makes more sense to me and many other pro screenwriters: Act 1 (pages 1 to 30), Act 2 (pages 31 to 60ish), Act 3 (61 to 85ish), Act 4 (86ish to 120ish).

If I were to sum up the four-act structure into a simple story, it would go like this:

Act 1

The Main Hero goes about his usual business with his sidekick, oblivious of his flaw. Suddenly, an incident occurs that will force him to eventually deal with that flaw. But since he doesn't want to face his flaw, or is in denial about it, he refuses to confront what the incident presented to him. Eventually he . . .

Here's how I break down the four acts (using *Skyfall* as an example):

ACT 1 *pages 1–30*	**ACT 2** *pages 31–60ish*	**ACT 3** *pages 61–85ish*	**ACT 4** *pages 86ish–120ish*

Setup Bond may be too old to kill the villian.	**The Quest's Escalating Complications** Bond's aging body gives out while trying to find the villian.	**Death Valley** Villian is going to kill Bond and the girl.	**Resolution** Bond kills the villain.

Act 2

. . . embarks on a quest that forces him to enter a "dark cave." The Main Hero, with the help of his Sidekicks, Maiden, Wise Old Man and Mother Figure, battles the Henchman, Shape-shifter, and Villain in this strange dark cave (who all challenge his flaw). Obstacles grow more difficult and complications escalate the deeper the Main Hero goes into the cave. It's at this point the Main Hero either sees a (false) light at the far end of the cave, or the cave collapses in front of him on his way toward the light. This collapse forces the Main Hero to find another way out.

Act 3

The Main Hero then experiences the darkest moments of his entire life as he continues to fight the Villain who prevents him from exiting the cave. In fact, the Main Hero reaches the lowest point he's ever experienced. Realizing that his only hope of getting out of the cave is to overcome his flaw *and* to face the Villain directly, the Main Hero prepares himself for battle. He then marches toward the Villain for a final, winner-take-all brawl.

Act 4

The Main Hero sacrifices his flaw completely on this final quest and suffers great pain because of it, but in doing so he defeats the Villain and finds a way out of the cave. Stepping into the sunlight, the Main Hero is rewarded with a new and better life. (Or, if he doesn't overcome his flaw, he is defeated and we, as an audience, learn from his failure.)

TURNING POINTS

Now that you've learned about the four-act structure, it's time to add Turning Points to your skill set. Turning Points are events that send the hero, and the story, into a dramatically different direction. A Turning Point happens on or near Minute 17 in Act One. Additional Turning Points occur in Acts 2 and 3 every fifteen minutes to keep the audience off guard, engaged, and guessing (Minutes 45, 60, and 75). Turning Points are also used during Minutes 90, 105, and 120 if you need to extend your story.

In fact, if you want to expand your story indefinitely, simply add a big Turning Point every fifteen minutes after Minute 120 — a Turning Point that will be difficult for the hero to unravel or resolve. This is a longtime secret trick of playwrights and screenwriters to extend any story.

The timeline below shows you when the Turning Points happen within the acts, which I will elaborate on when you reach that Minute in the book. The Inciting Incident, The Quest, Midpoint, and Final Quest are Turning Points, too, but they have their own special set of requirements, which I will also explain in more detail when you reach those Minutes.

Note: Check out the ultimate cheat sheet on pages 292–293 . . . the entire Beat by Beat structure summarized in a detailed timeline.

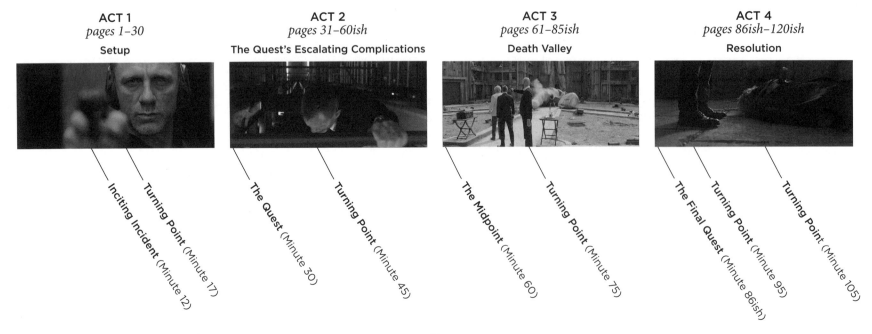

ACT 1
pages 1–30
Setup

ACT 2
pages 31–60ish
The Quest's Escalating Complications

ACT 3
pages 61–85ish
Death Valley

ACT 4
pages 86ish–120ish
Resolution

Inciting Incident (Minute 12)

Turning Point (Minute 17)

The Quest (Minute 30)

Turning Point (Minute 45)

The Midpoint (Minute 60)

Turning Point (Minute 75)

The Final Quest (Minute 86ish)

Turning Point (Minute 95)

Turning Point (Minute 105)

ACT 1

Setup

MINUTE 1

ATTENSION!

Tension begins

Whether it's action, adventure, comedy, drama, horror, or thriller, all successful movies start with *tension*: anxiety, apprehension, danger, discomfort, crisis, distress, hostility, or sexual tension. *Tension grabs attention.* One of the most popular tension-grabbers in film is *Danger.* When we witness something dangerous happening to others, our attention peaks because we feel we have to keep an eye on it for self-preservation. Five out of six of our case studies utilize Danger to start their stories:

Bond raises his gun.

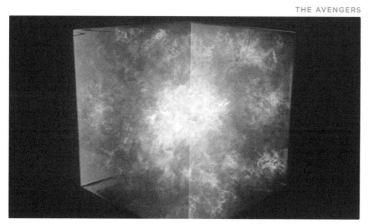

Narrator says: "What can the humans do but *burn*?"

Tracy can't reach her fiancé or his friends before the wedding.

Hansen shoots John an intimidating stare.

Teenage girl says: "It (the doll) was moving around by itself."

Nick narrates: "I picture cracking her lovely skull."

THE BUILD

Tension builds

Not only does . . .

Audience anticipation is increased by "building upon" already existing tension. Good screenwriters know that opening a story with tension will grab an audience, but just like in real life, if you don't escalate that tension, people will lose interest. A great way to help you escalate the tension in your story is to use the phrase, *Not only does*:

Not only does Bond want to stop the agent's bleeding, but M orders him to "Leave him!"

Not only does Nick Fury say "How bad is it?" to Coulson, Coulson responds with: "That's the problem, sir. We don't know."

Not only does Tracy tell Phil that: "We're getting married in five hours," but Phil responds with: "That's not gonna happen."

Not only does John overhear his fellow student say that MIT "is only taking one (candidate) this year, " but then he hears the student say: "Then things got worse . . ."

Not only does the doll move around by itself, but then: "Things got worse."

Not only does Nick ask Margo to pour him a bourbon, but Margo gives him a look that says: "This early in the morning?"

3

MINUTE 3

THE RATCHET

Tension builds even more

Not only that, but . . .

My dad taught me how to use a ratchet wrench when I was a teenager.
The ratchet was perfect for tightening bolts in small spaces, like inside the
engine block of my Chevy Nova. As the ratchet screwed the bolt closer
to the metal plate, I could feel the tension escalate in my wrist. We use
that same ratchet principle during Minutes 3 and 4. A great phrase to
help you build the tension even more is *Not only that, but now . . .*

Not only that, but now Bond and Eve ram into the fleeing car.

Not only that, but now Agent Hill tells Fury: "There might not be a minimum safe distance."

Not only that, but now Alan wears only a jockstrap in front of embarrassed Doug.

Not only that, but now Hansen acts as if John is the waiter.

Not only that, but now the possessed doll draws "Miss Me?" in red crayon.

Not only that, but now Nick gestures for a much-needed refill.

4

MINUTE 4

ANOTHER NOTCH

Tension ratchets up another notch

If you thought that was bad . . .

We're going to crank Minute 3's ratchet one more notch, which will not only
add more tension to our wrist, but will add more tension to our story. In
Star Wars, the stormtroopers burst through the door during this minute,
which ratchets the tension another notch, as it does in *Raiders of the Lost Ark*
when Indiana Jones's supposed ally pulls a gun on him. A phrase to help you
ratchet up the tension another notch is: *If you thought that was bad . . .*

If you thought that was bad, the enemy agent now shoots at Bond.

If you thought that was bad, Hawkeye now tells Fury the cube's doorways open from both sides.

If you thought that was bad, now Alan tells Doug: "I don't care if we kill someone."

If you thought that was bad, now John's loud, hungover new roommate arrives.

If you thought that was bad, now the thrown-out doll shows up in their closet.

If you thought that was bad, now the sexual tension heats up between Nick and Amy.

5

MINUTE 5

JAW DROPPER

Something extraordinary/astonishing happens

This minute makes the audience's jaws drop. The story seduces us even further by showing us something extraordinary or astonishing. Things that we don't see or hear every day fascinate us. It grabs our attention and dazzles us. What's the Jaw Dropper in *Jaws*? The shark rips the naked girl from the buoy and yanks her underneath the water permanently — an astonishing event in her life, to say the least, and for the audience.

The enemy agent crashes his motorcycle through a market window from a rooftop!

The Tesseract creates a giant door that the villain Loki enters Earth through.

Tracy's dad tells Doug: "What happens in Vegas stays in Vegas. Except for herpes. That shit'll come back with you."

John writes mathematical equations on the window.

"It's something demonic," Ed says.

Nick tells Amy: "I'm the guy to save you from all this awesomeness." (He basically proposes to her within a minute of meeting her.)

6

MINUTE 6

FRIEND OR FIST

Hero and ally bond or fight

These next two minutes are about establishing the hero and ally's relationship. This is a crucial step because the ally plays a big part in the hero's life later on. Because of this fact, we need to get to know him, and the hero, a bit better. Why? So we care what happens between them — and to them — further down the road. The best way to do this is by showing them either bonding (Friend) or fighting (Fist).

Eve follows Bond to help (Friend).

Fury and Hawkeye face off against Loki (Friend).

Doug, Phil, and Alan catch up in the car (Friend).

John and Charles get on each other's nerves (Fist).

Ed and Lorraine answer questions together at a lecture (Friend).

Nick kisses Amy and then gives her oral sex (Friend).

7

MINUTE 7

FRIEND OR FIST 2

Hero and/or ally bond or fight more

How do the hero and ally bond or fight even more in classic films? In *Raiders of the Lost Ark*, Indy saves his companion's life (Friend). In *Jaws*, Mrs. Brody tells her husband to be careful (Friend). In *The Sixth Sense*, Malcolm talks to his former patient in soothing tones (Friend). In *Forrest Gump*, Mama Gump scolds Forrest (Fist).

SKYFALL

Eve helps Bond corner the enemy agent (Friend).

THE AVENGERS

Fury and Selvig stand against Loki (Fist).

THE HANGOVER

Melissa fights with Stu over his Vegas trip (Fist).

A BEAUTIFUL MIND

John and Charles bond over booze (Friend).

THE CONJURING

Roger and Carolyn bond over their new home (Friend).

GONE GIRL

Nick and Margo play a game of Life while he tells her about his souring marriage (Friend).

8

MINUTE 8

SOMETHING STARTLING HAPPENS

A startling event occurs

Minute 8 startles somebody in the movie — mostly the hero — and in turn startles the audience. The audience needs a jolt here to keep them awake until the Inciting Incident happens during Minute 12. The Minute 8 startling event comes in all shapes and sizes . . .

Bond is shot!

Hawkeye shoots Fury!

Phil calls out to Stu (Melissa hears): "Paging Doctor Faggot!"

John shouts and calls his fellow students "lesser mortals."

The family dog refuses to enter their new home.

Nick discovers that his coffee table is smashed.

THE PURSUIT

Hero discovers something extraordinary/astonishing that must be pursued

The hero goes into pursuit mode here, and the audience will want to follow if you've properly addressed the steps leading to this minute. Whatever extraordinary thing the hero learns here, it prods him into action. His action peaks our curiosity — *What's going to happen next?*

Bond pursues the enemy agent with the earthmover.

Agent Hill discovers that Hawkeye turned traitor. She must stop him and Loki.

Alan says without irony: "That's why I managed to stay single this whole time," which prompts Stu to say: "Oh really, *that's* why you're single?"

John tries to find an algorithm for the random movement of pigeons.

April says to her sister: "Look what I found."

Nick discovers that Amy is not in the house. Where is she?

MINUTE 10

THE DISCUSSION

Someone important to the hero wants to discuss something significant

The Discussion draws in the audience. When someone important to us — either a lover, boss, parent, sibling, enemy, or friend — approaches us with a serious face and says, "I have something to discuss with you," it tweaks our interest. *What's this important thing they want to talk to me about?* Movie storytellers use this same real-life attention grabber during Minute 10 to keep us interested in their story.

M says to Bond: "What's going on? Report!"

Coulson tells Fury: "We're clear upstairs, sir. You need to go."

Phil asks Doug if Alan is "all there mentally."

Hansen asks John: "What if you never come up with your original idea?"

Roger and Carolyn's daughter tells Roger she didn't mean to break something in the (mysterious) closet.

Detective Rhonda asks Nick questions about his wife.

MINUTE 11

THE WARNING

Warning or threat is made

When a warning or threat is made to us in real life, we must address it immediately. If someone is threatening us, it could affect our lives in a major way. It could impact our finances, our health, our important relationships, or even our very existence. So it is for the audience, and why The Warning works in the next couple minutes.

Eve tells M: "There isn't much road. I don't think I can go any further."

Fury shoots at Loki.

Phil confronts Stu: "Don't you think it's strange that you have to lie about going to Vegas?"

Charles tells John: "You watched a mugging. That's weird."

Nancy tells her sister to shut up (after her sister tattles on her).

Detective Rhonda marks a spot that looks like blood.

INCITING INCIDENT

The Inciting Incident is a predicament that interrupts the Main Hero's ordinary routine during this time in his life — a predicament that will eventually lead to the exposure and testing of his flaw. Most times the Main Hero finds this predicament unsettling and fears it. In other cases, however, the predicament thrills the Main Hero — he sees it as an opportunity.

In all the successful movies I've researched, the Inciting Incident usually happens during Minute 12 (page 12 of your screenplay). The Inciting Incident lands on Minute 12 for all our successful case studies:

SKYFALL
Eve accidentally shoots Bond. The wound will test Bond's flaw — he may be getting too old to be an agent.

THE AVENGERS
The Tesseract ends up in the hands of hostile forces, which will ultimately test Tony Stark's flaw of selfishness.

THE HANGOVER
The guys enter Vegas, which will test Stu's flaw of accepting his girlfriend Melissa's bullying.

A BEAUTIFUL MIND
A classmate wants John to meet a girl. This will test John's flaw — his inability to connect fully with other people and (later) with his wife Alicia.

THE CONJURING
The dog barks a loud warning to the family. If the dog could speak he would be yelling: The house is full of evil entities! Run away! These entities will eventually test Lorraine's flaw — her deep-seated fear of demons.

GONE GIRL
Amy tells Nick that her mom's book character, Amazing Amy, is a better version of her (Amy). Nick takes Amy's side. This serious issue with Amy will test Nick's flaw — his chronic need to please people.

HARSHER WARNING

Harsher warning or threat is made

Someone can warn us, and it'll grab our attention, but if they amp up their threat or warning, we have no choice but to devote our full attention to the problem. The same is true in movie storytelling. For example, in *Top Gun,* the Chief *threatens* to demote Maverick. In *Spider-Man*, Osborn's assistant *warns* him not to do the test. In *Knocked Up,* the bartender yells at Ben: "Come on, Man!" — a *warning* not to take the beers. In *Jaws,* the mayor *warns* Brody not to put up the "No Swimming" signs.

Eve accidentally shoots Bond! He falls to his apparent death (a threat to national security).

Fury warns everyone that the Tesseract is with a hostile force.

Stu warns Doug that counting cards is illegal.

One of the guys wants John to meet a girl that's attracted to him (a threat to John's insecurity).

"I don't want any of you girls going down there," Roger warns.

Detective Rhonda discovers that Amy is "Amazing Amy" — a famous children's character (a threat to Nick's privacy).

THE SUBMISSION

Final warning/threat is made and the hero submits

Submission gains the audience's sympathy. We all react, subconsciously, when the hero submits. Why? Because we have been there ourselves. How many times have we tucked our tail between our legs and took it from a boss, a spouse, a teacher, a parent, or a traffic cop? It's humiliating. And when this happens to the hero, his weakness makes him real and gives us an extra reason to cheer for him. Hopefully, down the road, he'll overcome this weakness. And if he doesn't, we'll feel pity for him. Either way, we're on his side.

Bond's lifeless body goes over the waterfall.

A Russian general threatens Black Widow, who can't move — she's tied up in a chair.

After Stu fibs about being a doctor, Phil tells Stu: "You're a dentist. Don't try and get fancy." Doug looks at him, ashamed.

The woman slaps John. John gives up on her.

Carolyn to Roger: "You still too fried to christen the new house?" Roger submits: "Who said I'm fried?"

Amy's mother wants reluctant Amy to talk to the media. Amy (the hero in this scene) begrudgingly does.

MINUTE 14

DANGER WATCH

Docile hero watches danger approaching

The audience's heart rate elevates when they watch danger drawing closer. Once when I was a kid, my cousin Lisa and I hid in the back corner of a walk-in closet during a game of Hide and Seek. When my sister Wendy — the Seeker — opened the closet door and stepped inside to look for us, Lisa became so filled with anxiety when she saw my sister's sneakers stepping toward us that she screamed and gave up our hiding spot. Danger Watch builds anticipation the same way with the audience.

Seated M watches Mallory, her unhappy boss, step toward her.

Tied-up Black Widow watches the Russian general turn toward her with a torture tool.

Docile Stu doesn't want the room on his credit card (Melissa checks his statements).

The professor tells John he hasn't attended class or published any papers.

Carolyn sees a light shining in the basement . . .

Nick approaches Amy and asks her to marry him.

WHEW, THAT WAS CLOSE!

Hero experiences a close call while danger approaches

We've all had that moment when the tractor-trailer *almost* hit our car; or we almost fell down the steps; or a cop flicks on his lights, but then passes us to catch another speeder instead. We drag the back of our hands across our foreheads and say, *Whew, that was close!* The top movie screenwriters use this familiar real-life feeling to make the audience's hearts race faster.

Mallory wants M to retire early. She refuses and keeps her job. *Whew, that was close!*

A Russian thug grabs Black Widow. She defeats him. *Whew, that was close!*

Phil gestures to Stu: Why aren't you ready? Stu wraps up his phone call so they can leave. *Whew, that was close!*

John may not get placement, but he's still in the running. *Whew, that was close!*

The scary basement light is just Roger looking through junk. *Whew, that was close!*

Detective Rhonda has Nick examined and says: "Crossed off the list." Nick is probably not a suspect. *Whew, that was close!*

THE BIG CONCERN

Something causes deep concern for the hero or ally

The definition of The Big Concern is: *A troubled or anxious state of mind.* Whatever causes The Big Concern must be addressed *immediately,* which is a writer's secret weapon to slingshot the story forward. In *Raiders of the Lost Ark*, Indy shows concern when he learns that army intelligence has come to see him. In *Jaws*, Brody shows concern about going into the water. In *The Matrix*, Neo is concerned that he might go to jail.

SKYFALL

M is concerned over her near firing.

A BEAUTIFUL MIND

John is worried he might not get placement or recognition.

THE AVENGERS

Bruce Banner shows concern for the little girl's safety.

THE CONJURING

Concerned Carolyn says to Roger: "This clock stopped at 3:07 and so did the one in the hallway."

THE HANGOVER

Phil's concerned eyes stare at Stu's engagement ring.

GONE GIRL

(Seemingly) concerned Nick tells the detectives that they have a serious homeless problem in his neighborhood — they should check that out.

WORLD UPSIDE DOWN

Bad guy turns a good person's world upside down

The World Upside Down moment is when you've been minding your own business and someone comes along and ruins your day. A school bully trips you in the hall . . . a driver, not paying attention, smashes into your back bumper . . . a cop pulls you over for rolling through a stop sign. When the bad guy picks on someone on the big screen, it draws the audience's sympathy and we become even more invested in the story.

Someone has hacked into MI6 and burned M's image.

SHIELD finds Bruce Banner, who's been in hiding from them.

Phil tells Stu that Melissa is a complete bitch.

Charles yells at John and pushes him.

Carolyn and Roger find their dog dead.

"You haven't called your wife's parents?" Detective Rhonda asks Nick in an accusing tone.

TURNING POINT 17

Between Minutes 16–18, there's a big Turning Point in the story. To reiterate from this book's opening pages: Think of Turning Points as events that send the hero, or the story, into a dramatically different direction. Usually there's an attack on the hero or his ally during this minute, or an event embeds the hero deeper into his flaw, or a key member of the hero's core team is recruited (for Act 2's upcoming Quest).

SKYFALL
The Villain blows up MI6. (Minute 18)

THE AVENGERS
Black Widow recruits Bruce Banner to help SHIELD. (Minute 18)

THE HANGOVER
Stu informs the guys that he's going to ask (mean) Melissa to marry him. Phil calls Melissa a complete bitch and tries to talk Stu out of it. (Minute 17)

A BEAUTIFUL MIND
Charles pushes John's desk (and all his work) out the dorm window. (Minute 18)

THE CONJURING
Carolyn and Roger discover their beloved dog dead. (Minute 17)

GONE GIRL
Nick discovers that his father has been arrested. (Minute 18)

TROUBLE TURN

The event that will get the hero into trouble later

Trouble Turn is something that will get the hero deeper into a predicament. The deeper into trouble he gets, the more the audience feels for him. The more they feel for him, the more they'll follow him through every other twist and turn. In *Raiders of the Lost Ark*, Indy learns that Hitler wants the ark so he can obtain great power (which will get Indy into trouble later). In *Jaws*, the victim's bloody floating device washes ashore (which will soon get Chief Brody into trouble). In *Scream*, Casey discovers that two teenagers were brutally murdered (news that will affect her deeply later).

Someone blows up MI6's offices.

SHIELD wants Bruce Banner to help them.

Phil tells Stu that they can do whatever the fuck they want.

Charles pushes all John's work out the window.

Ed finds out that his daughter has snuck into the forbidden room to look at the possessed Annabelle doll.

Nick discovers that his dad is being booked in the jail.

19

MINUTE 19

THE THREAT

Bad guy, or secondary bad guys, make a threat/warning

The Threat, especially posed by a bad guy whose intent is to harm the hero, tweaks our audience's attention. Why is this? Because their sympathy for the hero has deepened by this point. They care what happens to him because of the sympathy we've established for him earlier. Let's look at the various types of bad guys who make threats during Minute 19.

A scorpion may sting Bond.

Black Widow pulls a gun on Bruce Banner when he yells: "Stop lying to me!"

Alan interrupts Phil. Phil glares at him.

When a girl looks at John, Hansen says: "He (John) may have the upper hand now, but wait till he opens his mouth."

The doors says: Demonology. Witchcraft. Danger!

Nick's dad tells him: "Get your fuckin' hands off me."

20

MINUTE 20

PUSH BACK

The hero pushes back in some way

Bad people or circumstances, to this point, have been pushing around the hero. Now it's time for him to push back. It shows that he has a bit of a backbone, which gains the audience's respect. They'll find themselves saying, "Good for you!" Most times *anger* is the emotion the hero evokes during the Push Back. The hero can also push back by *being contrary*, or *flirting back*, or by saying or doing something *shocking*.

Bond defeats the scorpion. Locals cheer Bond for his courage.

Fury wants The Avengers to help, which upsets the World Security Council.

Stu tells Phil: "We are definitely not supposed to be up here."

John makes the pretty girl smile.

Lorraine levels Ed with a gaze and says: "Stop blaming yourself."

Nick has sex with Amy in the library.

MINUTE 21

THE GREAT EFFECT

Something happens that greatly impacts the hero

The Great Effect not only impacts the hero, but it impacts the audience who's been cheering for him even harder since he showed he has a bit of a spine. What happens to the hero here can either have a positive impact, a negative impact, or be a double-edged sword (positive and negative combined).

— 70 —

Bond sees on the TV that MI6 was blown up.

Steve Rogers remembers the people he lost.

Alan slices his hand with a knife. Stu and the guys recoil.

John realizes that everyone will benefit if everyone does what's best for themselves *and* the group.

Roger hears creepy noises.

Margo scolds Nick for telling the police that Amy was "complicated."

22

MINUTE 22

TRUTH DECLARED

A truth is stated

This is the moment of truth, literally. It could be the bad guy, the hero, or the ally, but someone speaks a truth during Minute 22. Why is Truth Declared effective storytelling? Because in our everyday world, we're so inundated with white lies and fluff that when someone speaks the truth, our ears immediately perk up. Advertisers lie to us, politicians, salespeople. Sometimes even bosses, lovers, and friends tell us untruths. Because it is so rare, truth has power. And so it will be in your story and for your audience.

When asked by M where he's been, Bond replies: "Enjoying death."

Fury tells Steve Rogers that they're trying to save the world.

Phil says: "To a night the four of us will never forget."

John says that Adam Smith's long-held-to-be-true theory is wrong.

The oldest daughter tells Roger that Cindy is sleepwalking.

Margo and Nick say that Amy attracts drama.

23

MINUTE 23

SCARY STUFF

Hero experiences something scary with ally or love interest

When Scary Stuff happens to the hero and those he cares about, it scares the audience as well. Why? Because the hero is playing proxy for the audience by this point. They've put themselves in his shoes emotionally. The scariness amplifies in intensity over the next three minutes, for the hero *and* for the audience . . .

Bond tells M that maybe they've been playing the game too long.

Steve Rogers tells Fury that they should have left the Tesseract in the ocean.

Stu and Alan wake up in a severe stupor.

John waits to see what Professor Helinger thinks of his paper.

Roger sees Cindy banging her head against the wall.

Detective Rhonda is told that the splatters in the kitchen are, indeed, blood.

24

MINUTE 24

SCARY STUFF 2

Hero and/or ally/love interest experience more scary stuff

During Minute 24, the scariness amps up a notch to hold our audience's attention, like it does in *The Godfather* when Don Corleone tells his nephew to act like a man (the Godfather's sudden anger scares Johnny). In *Knocked Up*, Alison thinks that she might be pregnant (scary situation for a single girl). In *Die Hard*, the bad guys fire guns near the employees, which scares them. In *The Matrix*, Trinity pulls out a scary contraption and presses it onto Neo's navel.

Tanner tells Bond that someone hacked into "everything."

Jarvis tells Tony Stark that SHIELD is on the line, which Stark wants no part of.

Alan encounters a tiger in the bathroom.

Displeased Hansen approaches John.

Roger sees another bruise on Carolyn's body.

Nick and Margo drive to the courthouse for the press conference.

25

MINUTE 25

SCARY STUFF 3

Hero and/or ally/love interest experience even more scary stuff

In our trilogy of scary minutes, the scariness escalates, as it does in *Jaws* when Brody studies his scary shark book even more, or in *Forrest Gump* when Jenny places Forrest's hand on her breast (scary for him because he's never had sex). In *Die Hard*, the head of the bad guys, Hans Gruber, speaks in threatening tones to the scared employees.

Tanner tells Bond that he'll be meeting with Mallory, the man who tried to fire M.

Jarvis tells Stark that SHIELD *insists* they speak with him, which he wants no part of.

Stu discovers that he's missing a tooth.

John is shown a complicated code from Moscow.

Roger finds a dying pigeon next to the house.

Nick faces the press.

26

MINUTE 26

THE BIG UNEXPECTED

Something big and unexpected occurs

A classic example of The Big Unexpected is when Indiana Jones enters Marion's bar. She laughs, brushes off her hands and says, "Indiana Jones, I always knew some day you'd come walking back through my door." We think everything is cool between them, so does Indy, when suddenly she *punches* him in the face! Big and unexpected! Before this minute we experienced three minutes straight of scary tension. There has to be an unexpected moment here to keep the audience off balance.

Bond collapses after taking his physical.

John breaks the complicated code and shows the General the enemy's entry points.

Coulson/SHIELD shows up in Stark's apartment unannounced.

Carolyn hears April talking to someone who isn't there.

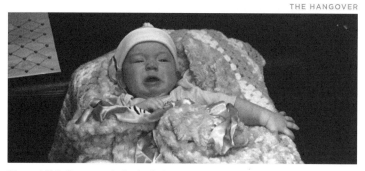

Stu and Phil discover a baby in their suite.

Nick smiles for the media's pictures — an unexpected reaction for a worried husband.

MINUTE 27

THE MINI-QUEST

A Mini-Quest happens just before the Big Quest

Now that we've jolted the audience, let's take them on a Mini-Quest before Act 2's Big Quest begins. This Mini-Quest involves something that is immediately important to the hero or ally. The Mini-Quest's undertone is urgency. Examples of the Mini-Quest in classic movies are when Indy tells Marion that he needs the bronze medallion (Indy's Mini-Quest before searching for the ark). In *Jaws*, the fisherman tries to swim to shore before the shark eats him (the fisherman's Mini-Quest before all the fishermen try to capture the shark). In *Top Gun*, Maverick must defeat the instructor during the first training exercise (Maverick's Mini-Quest before battling the real bad guys).

SKYFALL

Bond attempts to hit the bullseye.

THE AVENGERS

Coulson tries to convince Stark to join The Avengers.

THE HANGOVER

The guys try to figure out what to do with the baby.

A BEAUTIFUL MIND

John asks who "Big Brother" is.

THE CONJURING

April to Carolyn: "Can we play Hide and Clap?"

GONE GIRL

The detectives want to know about Amy's former boyfriend.

BIG QUEST PREP

Hero prepares for the bigger quest with ally

Now that the Mini-Quest has been taken care of, or has just about been taken care of, it's time for the hero to make preparations for Act 2's Big Quest. And if you've done your job correctly up to this point, the audience will follow the hero on this bigger quest. They'll want to know how he'll fare in this new endeavor. The Big Quest Prep develops over the next two minutes . . .

Bond takes a psychological exam with MI6's psychologist.

Stark studies the information Coulson gave him about the Tesseract situation.

Phil grabs a paper and pen.

John prepares for their latest assignment with Sol and Bender.

Carolyn hears a clap in the dresser. She tries to figure out who made the noise.

Nick and Detective Rhonda discuss "Clue One" that Amy left behind.

BIG QUEST PREP 2

Hero and/or ally's preparation for bigger quest continues

Big Quest Prep continues, almost as if the story is accelerating up a ramp, ready to propel the hero into Act 2. Maverick defeats his instructor in *Top Gun*'s training drill (in preparation to deal with the real enemy). In *Knocked Up*, Alison and Ben meet in a restaurant to talk, preparing themselves to deal with the pregnancy. Morpheus offers Neo the red or blue pill (preparing him to see The Matrix).

Bond gives the bullet shrapnel from his chest to forensics.

Coulson tells Steve Rogers that they've made some modifications to his suit.

Phil writes down a list of what they remember.

Sol and Bender remind John that he has to teach MIT class.

Something pulls on Christine's foot. What was it?

Nick and Detective Rhonda find Clue Two.

THE NEED

A need is shown or expressed

The definition of The Need is: *A condition requiring relief; anything that is necessary but lacking.* When we have a need in our life, whether it's to buy some fast food because we're starving, or a need to be on time for a job interview, or a need to pursue a love interest, that need becomes our main focus. When the characters in our story express a need, we pay attention because we know the feeling oh too well.

SKYFALL

Bond glances at his watch and paces — he needs to have a meeting with M.

A BEAUTIFUL MIND

The students express a need to have the window open.

THE AVENGERS

Loki needs to rule the world.

THE CONJURING

Christine needs to know what pulled on her foot.

THE HANGOVER

Stu needs to know: "What the hell is going on?"

GONE GIRL

Nick needs to shut off the blaring security system.

ACT 1
CHECKLIST

- Is your Main Hero orphaned in some way?

- Did you clearly define your Main Hero's flaw?

- Does your Main Hero have a redeeming quality (kind to animals, children, or elderly people, or highly skilled at something)?

- Have you clearly defined who all your archetypes will be?

- Have you introduced the Inciting Incident around Minute 12 (Page 12 of your screenplay)?

- Have you clearly defined your theme? Do all your archetypes represent a different angle to the theme? Does your dialogue reflect the theme?

THE QUEST

Your Main Hero is going to enter a new world that will be disorienting and will test his flaw in escalating conflicts. Despite his floundering, he commits to a plan of action to achieve his goal. Soon after, he battles his flaw as he attempts to figure out who his allies and enemies are in this strange new domain.

The Quest usually kicks in between Minutes 29 to 35 (try to land it on Minute 30 for tighter storytelling).

Here are the Quests for our case studies:

SKYFALL
Mallory sends Bond back into the field to "find the list." (Minute 33)

THE AVENGERS
The aircraft carrier launches. The Avengers set off to find the Tesseract. (Minute 33)

THE HANGOVER
Stu and the guys set out to figure out "what the hell is going on." (Minute 30)

A BEAUTIFUL MIND
John agrees to help the Department of Defense crack Russian codes. (Minute 35)

THE CONJURING
Carolyn finds out the evil entity wants her family dead. She wants to save her family from harm (this affects the Main Hero Lorraine who will have to confront the entity and her fear of them). (Minute 34)

GONE GIRL
Nick goes on a quest to find out what Amy's third clue means — the clue he hides from the detectives. (Minute 31)

ACT 2

The Quest's Escalating Complications

MINUTE 31

DISTRESS SIGNAL

Hero sees/hears something that distresses him

Distress drops by for a visit. And since movies are sight and sound, the hero either *sees* or *hears* something that distresses him, which sends out a Distress Signal to our proxy-audience. The Distress Signal happens over and over in blockbusters, like in *Raiders of the Lost Ark* when Indy *sees* the red-hot poker moving toward Marion's face, or in *Jaws* when Brody *sees* the mutilated body, or in *Die Hard* when John *sees* that Hans is about to shoot Takagi.

Bond sees Mallory enter, the man who could fire him.

The Chitauri leader warns Loki (the hero in this scene) not to fail.

The guys see Doug's mattress speared on a roof statue.

John sees one of his female students addressing the window/noise issue — an issue he failed to resolve on his own.

Christine sees her door moving.

Nick reads Amy's Clue Three that he hid from the detectives.

32

ANXIETY AMP

Sought-after truth or object is revealed and causes great anxiety

"Be careful what you wish for" applies during the Anxiety Amp. In
Minute 32, the revelation the hero sought after is found and amps up
his anxiety (and the audience's anxiety). In *Raiders of the Lost Ark*,
Indy and the Nazi's shoot at each other over the medallion. In *Jaws*, an
anxious Hooper says, "This was no boat accident, it was a shark!"

Bond wonders if he passed the tests.

John wanted to know who "Big Brother" was. He's about to find out.

Learning that he can't hide if he fails amps Loki's anxiety.

Christine sees someone standing behind the door.

Phil turns on the cop car light. Stu panics.

Nick slams his fist on the horn after reading Amy's Clue Three.

33

MINUTE 33

OMINOUS OH NO

Hero sees/does/hears something ominous

The definition of the Ominous Oh No is: *The foreshadowing of evil or tragic developments; potentially harmful or having an injurious effect.* Seeing, hearing, or doing something ominous seem to be the most popular ways to relay this menacing feeling to the audience during Minute 33 . . .

Mallory tells Bond: "Don't cock it up."

Steve Rogers sees that the aircraft carrier is doing something strange.

The doctor tells the guys that they came in with concussions, bruised ribs, and were "whacked out of their minds."

Parcher leads John toward the "abandoned building."

Christine tells Nancy: "It's (the ghost is) standing right behind you."

Amy tells Nick that her parents need all her trust fund money. They're broke.

34

FRIEND EFFECT

Ally's behavior impacts the hero

On page 34 of your script, the ally does something that directly affects your hero. This is either expressed in words or deeds, like when Goose tells Maverick he hopes they graduate Top Gun, or in *Star Wars* when Obi-Wan talks about the Dark Side, which troubles Luke. Here's how our case studies apply the Friend Effect to either test or help the hero . . .

SKYFALL

M tells Bond, with confidence: "You are ready for this."

A BEAUTIFUL MIND

Parcher tells John: "What I'm about to tell you could lead to imprisonment."

THE AVENGERS

"Is this a submarine?" Rogers asks. "No," Banner replies, "this is much worse."

THE CONJURING

Carolyn tells Roger: "(the demon) wants my family dead."

THE HANGOVER

The doctor informs Stu and Phil that they were given a date rape drug.

GONE GIRL

Amy sees that Nick is playing videogames instead of working, and points it out to him.

BAIT AND SWITCH

Seems like this new world is positive, but is it really?

The Bait and Switch affects the audience because things seem hunky-dory, peachy keen, aces up, but then there's a dark undercurrent that keeps them off balance. For example, in *The Matrix,* Neo is welcomed to the real world (+), but he's stuck with hundreds of acupuncture needles (–).

After M just told Bond that he's ready (+), Tanner says privately to M: "Did he (Bond) pass the test?" M: "He didn't." (−)

Suspicious Banner says to Fury: "Thank you for asking nicely (+). How long am I staying?" (−)

The guys learn from the doctor that they just came from a wedding (+), but whose? (−)

Parcher tells John that he's the best natural code breaker he's ever seen (+), but the job will be dangerous (−).

Ed and Lorraine joke around (+), but Ed doesn't want her going with him to see about a demon (−).

Nick sees that the whole community is helping to find Amy (+), but some look at him with accusing eyes (−).

HIDE AND SEEK

Main object of desire stays hidden

This minute entices the audience with something I spoke about earlier; something that goes back to our childhood: Hide and Seek. Your friends hid and you searched for them. We desired to discover where they were hidden. Magicians manipulate this same desire in their tricks. They make an object or an audience member disappear. The audience waits in anticipation until he brings the object, or audience member, back. Top-notch screenwriters perform the same prestidigitation during Minute 36.

Q keeps Bond's ticket and gun hidden in his jacket pockets.

Coulson says they are: "sweeping every accessible camera on the planet" for the Tesseract.

The chapel owner recognizes the guys, but *why* were they there the night before? And where's Doug?

The Russian codes are hidden somewhere in the periodicals.

Carolyn goes looking for who is hiding and clapping.

Nick spots Amy's former boyfriend, but he disappears before he can talk to him.

37

MINUTE 37

OVER HIS HEAD

Hero or ally realizes he may be in over his head

How many times have we found ourselves Over Our Heads in life? We immediately flail our arms and kick our feet to reach the water's surface before we drown. We can feel this way in a new job, relationship, or in any number of unfamiliar situations. So it is for our hero and audience during this minute.

After young, computer-savvy Q leaves, Bond says sarcastically to himself: "Brave new world" (he may be over his head in this new youth-oriented MI6).

Fury says to Steve Rogers: "You're up." Rogers takes a hesitant breath (he may be in over his head in this new situation).

Stunned Stu discovers that he married a stranger (he's engaged to someone else).

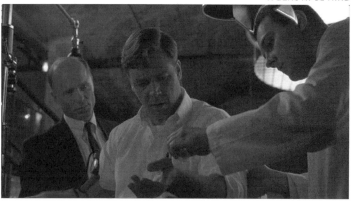

Parcher plants radium in John's arm. "So what am I now," John asks with concern, "a spy?"

Carolyn notices that something knocked her family's photos off the wall.

Nick's fan turns on him after he asks her to delete their selfie together.

38

MINUTE 38

POSITIVE RECONNECT

Hero reconnects with ally in a positive way

We all need positive reinforcement from our friends; so does the hero. But the Positive Reconnect is the screenwriter's way of luring the audience into a false sense of security. Deep down we know the good times can't last. Something bad will interrupt the hero again, but we don't know exactly when, which creates anticipation.

MI6 gives Bond his flight number. They still have confidence in him.

Steve Rogers looks at his Captain America suit. He's ready for action.

Phil tells Stu that the girl he married might know where Doug is.

Alicia says she solved John's equation.

Carolyn turns on the light (her ally in this situation).

Amy's mother apologizes to Nick after scolding him.

NEW JOURNEY BOND

Hero bonds further with main ally on new journey

In the previous minute, the hero reconnected with the ally in a positive way, but now, to keep the story moving forward, there must be a new journey that propels them into action, like in *Knocked Up* when Ben and Alison agree to keep the baby, or in *Pulp Fiction* when Vincent drinks Mia's shake while she looks at him with desire (they are starting a new journey together as possible lovers). The hero may bond with inanimate objects as well, like James Bond does with his new Walther PPK in *Skyfall*, or Carolyn does with the lights in *The Conjuring*.

Bond and his new Walther PPK follow the enemy agent in Singapore.

Loki (the hero in this scene) turns into his true self and is ready to rule the world.

Alan tells Stu he'll help him burn the cop car and all the evidence.

Alicia asks John out on a date.

Carolyn turns on more lights as she explores who is clapping.

Margo and Nick discuss what to do about people's perception of him.

40

MINUTE 40

ALLY'S WORLD

We learn more about the ally and their world

During this minute, the focus is taken off the hero and we get a glimpse
into the ally's world. Since the ally is key in the hero's life, we need to let
the audience know them a little better. There are a number of reasons for
this. The writer wants us to: 1) like the ally (so we approve of the hero being
with them); 2) fear for the ally (to understand what the hero goes through
if the ally is put into danger); 3) understand what the ally is capable of
(which will play out later in the story); 4) have a clearer understanding of
the ally and their world (so we know what the hero is dealing with).

— 110 —

Bond activates his hand-coded Walther PPK that only he can shoot.

Loki's scepter (his ally) can blow up police cars.

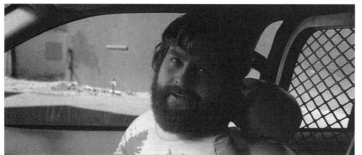

Alan says, to everyone's shock: "It would be so cool if I could breastfeed."

Alicia tells John that she's a painter.

The basement light (Carolyn's ally) reveals that there's something alive down there.

Margo wishes their mom was here.

41

MINUTE 41

THORNY ROSE

Things may seem kinda rosy, but there's still ugliness out there

During this minute we feel a moment of positive relief for the hero (the rose), but then he's immediately pricked with a thorn — a problem he must solve. In *Jaws*, Hooper interrupts the lovely dinner (rose) to tell Brody that the shark is still out there (thorn). In *Juno*, Mark composes lucrative music for commercials (rose), but Juno calls him a sellout (thorn).

As Bond follows the enemy agent into the luxurious building (rose), he passes the security guards that the agent has killed (thorn).

Loki tells the people that their lives will be better if they follow him (rose), but then he raises his scepter to kill an old man (thorn).

While Stu tells Melissa over the phone that things are fine (rose), a stranger bashes their windshield (thorn).

John is having fun on his date (rose), but he sees men watching him (thorn).

The oldest daughter was sleeping soundly (rose), but is awakened by Cindy banging her head against the wall (thorn).

Nick and Amy move to Missouri (rose), but she wishes he would have asked first (thorn).

42

MINUTE 42

SURPRISE REVEAL

Ally/Hero reveals something surprising

Our ears perk up when our friends tell us something surprising, don't they? Same trick works in storytelling, which is used during Minute 42 to reel in the audience. Sometimes the Surprising Reveal is a negative surprise, sometimes positive, as we'll see in the following examples . . .

Bond's (wounded) arm gives way while holding onto the elevator.

Captain America flings his shield, which strikes Loki.

Stu's stranger-wife gives him a surprise passionate kiss.

Alicia tells John that she tried to count all the stars. She made it to 4,348.

The oldest daughter shows fear for the first time.

Nick's girlfriend shows up at Margo's place — he's been having an affair.

43

MINUTE 43

SURPRISE REVEAL 2

Ally reveals something even more surprising

What if your friend, who just revealed something surprising to you, followed up with something even *more* surprising? We'd be riveted and would want to know more. So will the audience. Death, or the mention of possible death, seems to be a popular surprise reveal during Minute 43.

Drawing his Walther PPK, Bond sees the enemy agent cutting a hole in the high rise window.

Iron Man's explosives drive Loki backwards.

Stu's new wife is wearing his grandmother's Holocaust ring.

Alicia wants John sexually.

The oldest daughter rolls on the floor as if something is attacking her.

Nick's girlfriend is much younger than him.

44

MINUTE 44

NEW NEWS

Hero reacts to new news

During this minute the hero either reacts to last minute's surprise, like Indiana Jones does in *Raiders of the Lost Ark* (by drinking heavily after Marion's death), or the hero reacts to new news during this minute, like Don Corleone does in *The Godfather* when he sees two armed men approaching him. Here's how our case studies react to New News:

Bond realizes that the enemy agent is going to shoot somebody in the neighboring building. He wonders if he should intervene.

After seeing Thor grab Loki, Captain America says: "That guy's a friendly?"

Surprised Stu learns that his new wife is a stripper/escort.

John sees code patterns emerging in the newspapers and magazines.

Ed reacts to his students' overwhelming response.

Nick's girlfriend takes off her shirt. He starts foreplay.

OUT OF THE ORDINARY

Hero does something brave and out of the ordinary for him

This is the minute we see another side of the hero — something Out of the Ordinary. It's a moment when the hero shows courage. This moment makes us respect the hero on a subconscious level because we admire people who show this quality. Why? Because stepping out of your comfort zone is extremely difficult to do. If they can do it, maybe the audience can too.

Bond allows the enemy agent to kill his target.

Captain America leaps from the plane.

Stu waits at the police station to be processed.

John types in the code imbedded in his arm.

Carolyn attends a ghost hunter talk.

Amy says that Nick uses her for sex.

TURNING POINT 45

Between Minutes 44–47, there's another big Turning Point. Keep in mind that major Turning Points happen in the middle of the story — Acts 2 and 3 — every fifteen minutes to keep the audience off guard, engaged, and guessing (Minutes 30, 45, 60, and 75).

Usually someone attacks the hero during this Turning Point, as happens in *The Avengers, The Hangover,* and *A Beautiful Mind*, which you'll see below. Other times something surprising is revealed that will send the hero down a wildly different path, as in *The Conjuring* and *Gone Girl*.

SKYFALL
Bond witnesses Silva's henchman assassinate someone important. Bond and the henchman try to kill each other. (Minute 45)

THE AVENGERS
Thor shows up in a dramatic lightning storm, attacks the Avengers, and kidnaps Loki. (Minute 45)

THE HANGOVER
Cops burst through the door and arrest the guys. (Minute 44)

A BEAUTIFUL MIND
John becomes certain that he's being followed. (Minute 44)

THE CONJURING
Lorraine begs the Warrens to come to her house. "I'm so afraid this thing wants to hurt us," she pleads. It's the first time the Warrens and Lorraine meet. This meeting will change the course of both their lives. (Minute 46)

GONE GIRL
Nick has sex with a young student whom he's been secretly dating. (Minute 44)

46

MINUTE 46

THE REVELATION

Something significant is revealed

Revelations, doled out bit by bit, are like clues left on a trail leading somewhere interesting for the audience. The Revelation comes in four different forms during Minute 46: 1) Revelations that rock the hero's world; 2) Revelations about the ally; 3) Revelations about the hero; 4) Revelations about the bad guy.

The woman in the other room has seen Bond.

Someone drives by and looks at John. They are watching him.

Loki tells Thor: "I remember a shadow. Living in the shade of your greatness."

Carolyn tells Ed and Lorraine: "I have five daughters who are scared to death."

A cop reveals that they found the guys' Mercedes parked in the middle of Las Vegas Blvd.

Amy tells Nick she wants a baby.

47

MINUTE 47

THE ESCORT

Ally takes, or will take, the hero somewhere

One of the functions of the ally, especially during Minute 47, is to lead the hero somewhere. This action drives the hero, and the story, forward into fresh territories, like in *Jaws* when Hooper *takes* Brody out into the ocean at night, or in *Raiders of the Lost Ark* when Sallah says he will *take* Indy to the old man, and in *The Matrix* when Tank says he will *take* Neo to his training.

Bond finds a clue that will lead him closer to the list.

Iron Man forces Thor away from Loki.

The cop tells the guys that he will take them to see the judge Monday morning.

Alicia takes John on a picnic.

Carolyn takes Lorraine to meet her daughters.

Detective James accompanies Detective Rhonda into a crack area.

48

MINUTE 48

NEEDED KNOWLEDGE

Ally gives/shows hero needed knowledge

The next three minutes are devoted to giving the hero *knowledge*. The knowledge the ally gives the hero (and the audience) during Minute 48 aids the hero's goal or situation, or shows him what he needs to do next. You'll also notice that during these three minutes the knowledge becomes more and more ominous as the minutes progress . . .

M says: "(The hacker has) posted the first five names. Get them out now."

Iron Man tells Thor: "He (Loki) gives up the cube, he's all yours."

Stu asks Phil: "What are you getting at?" Phil tries to get them out of their situation with the cops.

Alicia kisses John — she accepts him for who he is.

Rogers tells Ed that the banging noises come in threes. Ed says it's an insult to the trinity.

Crack addict/informant tells Detective Rhonda that Amy wanted a gun.

FOREBODING FACT

Hero is given more knowledge/warning, often ominous

During this minute, a dark undertone accompanies the Needed
Knowledge the hero learned in the previous minute. For example,
during Minute 49 in *The Godfather*, Tom is told that Don Corleone
is dead. In *Forrest Gump*, Forrest discovers that Lt. Dan is wounded.
Here are the Foreboding Facts in our case studies:

SKYFALL

Eve tells Bond that the enemy has broken the encryption. British agents' lives are in danger.

THE AVENGERS

Iron Man turns Thor's power against him.

THE HANGOVER

The cop tasers Stu.

A BEAUTIFUL MIND

Charles tells John that his sister died in a car crash.

THE CONJURING

Lorraine hears screaming noises in the basement.

GONE GIRL

Margo saw Nick with the young girl and calls him a fuckin' idiot.

50

MINUTE 50

THE PORTENT

Something potentially deadly is seen or explained

Portent means: *An indication that something calamitous may occur*. The knowledge given during this minute is laced with possible danger or even death. In *Raiders of the Lost Ark*, Sallah spots the dead monkey and catches the poisoned date before Indy eats it. In *Little Miss Sunshine*, the literary agent informs Richard that his book deal fell through — his dream is dead. In *Juno*, Juno tells us that Paulie's mom doesn't like her (deadly to her and Paulie's relationship).

SKYFALL

Bond hands Eve his razor.

A BEAUTIFUL MIND

John asks Charles if he should marry Alicia. "How do you know for sure?"

THE AVENGERS

Captain America strikes Thor in the head with his shield.

THE CONJURING

April tells Lorraine that something bad happened to her imaginary friend Rory.

THE HANGOVER

The boy who Alan kicked at earlier volunteers to taser him.

GONE GIRL

Margo tells Nick that he's "a liar and a cheat just like Dad."

51

MINUTE 51

THE ENGAGE

Hero and/or ally engage the enemy, the enemy intimidates the hero

Now that the hero has his knowledge, or has been warned, the enemy shows up — I call the moment The Engage. It's where they mix it up for a bit, like fighters in a ring feeling each other out, testing each other's endurance for the remaining rounds. And the enemy shows up for the next three minutes:

Bond looks at the dragon he's about to enter.

Loki grins at Banner.

The cop tasers Alan until he collapses.

John is late again for dinner. Alicia glares at him.

Lorraine sees a ghost in the mirror.

Margo shows Nick the TV news, which makes him out to be a bad guy.

52

MINUTE 52

SAY UNCLE

Pressure is applied to the hero or ally

When I was a kid, bullies would seize weaker classmates, put them into headlocks, and make them to say "Uncle" before releasing them. The phrase originated from the similar sounding Irish word "anacol," which means "an act of mercy or quarter." The experience was always humiliating for the victim. That's why the phrase is fitting for Minute 52. Not only does the enemy intimidate the hero in the previous minute, now he almost defeats him, which draws even more sympathy from the audience.

Bond tells Eve over his headset: "I've got three exits, lots of blind spots."

John wants to ask Alicia to marry him, but the notion unsettles him.

Loki tells Fury: "It burns you to have come so close . . . to have the Tesseract; to have power."

Lorraine sees a dead body dangling behind Ed (which overwhelms her).

Grief overcomes Alan because Doug might be dead.

The TV show host calls Nick a sociopath, which stuns him.

53

MINUTE 53

THE INTIMIDATION

Enemy intimidates hero

In the Old Testament story of David and Goliath, the Philistine's nine-foot-tall super-soldier stood on the opposing hillside and hurled taunts at the much smaller Israelite soldiers. He did this to intimidate them; to show them who's boss. The bad guy uses this same intimidation against the hero during Minute 53. And sometimes the bad guy is simply *life*.

The bodyguard stares at Bond.

Thor tells The Avengers that Loki has an army.

A man leaps out of the trunk and attacks Phil.

John weighs Alicia's data and wonders if he should marry her, or if she will marry him.

Lorraine tells Roger and Carolyn that a dark entity has latched onto their family and is feeding off them.

A detective states that it's Amy's blood all over the kitchen.

54

MINUTE 54

THE LIGHTBULB

New positive or negative revelation is made

Another revelation is made during this minute — a lightbulb blinks on in the mind. The lightbulb will either illuminate something positive or negative. Whichever one it is, you must reveal something here to keep the audience interested in your story, as in *Raiders of the Lost Ark* when Indy discovers that the sun's rays work through the medallion (positive revelation), or when Jester surprises Maverick with an unexpected attack in *Top Gun* (negative revelation).

The woman recognizes Bond (negative revelation).

Stark says that the portal can open as wide or as long as Loki wants (negative revelation).

Stu says he has internal bleeding (negative revelation).

Alicia and John marry (positive revelation).

Ed explains that the church has to authorize a new exorcism (negative revelation).

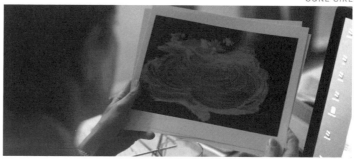

The police photos indicate "blunt force" (negative revelation).

55

MINUTE 55

SIDESWIPE

The hero or ally is sideswiped in some way, either positively or negatively

It's time to give the hero, and the audience, another jolt. When I was sixteen, I pulled my car onto Pennsylvania's Route 22 and a silver van sideswiped my Nova at 60 mph. That same year a cute neighbor girl I secretly liked kissed me unexpectedly while we sat on her porch. Both moments seized my attention, to say the least. Movies use this same sideswipe moment to elevate our adrenaline levels and keep us glued to the screen.

Severine wants Bond to have a drink with her.

Stark offers a rare compliment to Banner.

Alan confesses that he drugged them.

Russians shoot at Parkin and John.

Carolyn's voice didn't record on the tape machine.

Nick lies to the crowd — calls Amy his "soulmate."

56

MINUTE 56

DARK TWIST CHAT

Hero talks with a friend, and then there's a dark twist

We're having a pleasant chat with a friend outside a grocery store. We're about to wrap up the conversation and finish our errands when he says, "Oh, did you hear that your brother-in-law was arrested?" That's the Dark Twist Chat. Suddenly we forget about our errands. We want to know more. The writer uses this same technique to make the audience forget about the outside world and keep their attention focused on the movie . . .

Eve tells Bond over his earpiece that the woman is pretty. Bond drops his earpiece in Eve's drink.

Captain America tells Fury that they should start with Loki's scepter. Fury responds: "It is powered by the cube."

Stu tells Phil and Alan: "Our best friend Doug is probably face-down in a ditch right now with a meth-head butt-fucking his corpse."

Parcher tells John to stay back, and then he fires a gun.

Lorraine tells Ed the house's history. The original owner's wife sacrificed a baby there.

Nick spots his girlfriend in the crowd. She mouths the word "asshole" to him.

57

MINUTE 57

DIFFICULT WORDS

Difficult question/request/statement is asked/made

The posing of a difficult question, request, or statement within a scene keeps us turning pages. A difficult question, request, or statement *has* to be dealt with in some way. And "dealing with it" drives the story forward. For example, my friend's parents once gathered him and his sisters into the den one night. Once everyone was settled, his dad told them he and his mom were getting a divorce. These Difficult Words caused immediate emotional upheaval within the siblings. Storytellers borrow the tension created in such moments to spark life into their movie minutes.

Severine says to Bond: "I am correct in assuming that you killed Patrice?"

Captain America tells Stark: "Threatening the safety of everyone on this ship isn't funny."

Alan: "What about the tiger? What if he got out?"

Alicia asks John where he was. He can't tell her that he was almost killed.

Rory's mother killed herself in the cellar.

Detective Rhonda asks Nick if he knew Amy was pregnant.

58

MINUTE 58

VITAL EVENT

A vital event happens to the hero or ally

The Vital Event can be portrayed in a number of ways: Something alters the hero's life (in *Knocked Up*, the guys find out that there's already a mrskin.com — their website is screwed!); it touches upon the past (in *Top Gun*, Maverick stares at his dead father's picture); information is explained (in *Star Wars*, Tarkin says he will blow up Alderaan); it reveals the state of a relationship (in *The Godfather*, Michael can't tell Kate that he loves her); or it poses a threat (in *Scream*, Billy threatens Randy).

Severine asks Bond if he can kill "him."

Banner wonders why SHIELD is in the energy business.

Mike Tyson punches Alan in the face.

John's paranoia elevates. He walks out on his class.

Ed and Lorraine's tape recorder plays demonic sounds at 3:07 a.m.

The detectives accuse Nick of murdering Amy.

THE DECEPTION

A deceit occurs

Robert Southey once wrote that deception is "a lie reduced to practice." When we witness someone deceiving another person in real life, it creates immediate suspicion within us. Again, it goes back to self-preservation: If he deceives her, will he also deceive me? Deception can threaten our relationships, our jobs, and ultimately, our security. But deception isn't entirely bad in some cases. When the hero uses deception to "put one over" on the bad guy, we admire his cleverness. Here are a number of ways characters deceive each other in movies:

Severine pretends for the bodyguards that she's deceiving Bond.

Stark and Banner wonder what SHIELD is hiding.

Mike Tyson's friend gives the guys Doug's jacket that he had been holding.

Parcher sneaks up on John. He's been following him.

Ed sets up a camera to secretly take a picture.

Nick says that he did not buy all the items on his credit card statement — "This is identity theft!"

60

MINUTE 60

THE SHOCKER

Something shocks the hero or ally

During the one-hour mark, we experience The Shocker: something that draws a swift inhalation of breath from the audience. And it either happens to the hero or his allies, as it does in *Star Wars* when Tarkin blows up Alderaan, or when the teenager shows Cole the back of his blown-out skull in *The Sixth Sense*.

Bond falls into the pit with the beast.

Stark tells Banner that the Hulk probably saved his life.

The guys put roofies in the tiger's red meat.

Parcher won't allow John to quit.

Sudden images flash in Lorraine's mind when she touches Carolyn's photo.

Margo calls Nick out for lying about not wanting kids.

ACT 2 CHECKLIST

- Have you kept your dialogue and scenes centered around your theme?
- Have you escalated the Main Hero's complications in his life?
- What are the worst things that could happen to your Main Hero? Are you making them happen to him in your script (saving the worst for Act 3)?
- Have your Main Hero's Sidekicks, Maiden, and Villain or Henchman tested your Hero's flaw?

THE MIDPOINT

This is the Midpoint in your story. The Midpoint's "Cave Collapse" or "False Light" (as I refer to them) usually happens between Minutes 55 and 65. Here's how the Midpoint in our case studies play out:

SKYFALL
Bond falls into the pit occupied by a deadly creature. The bodyguard readies himself to kill fallen Bond (Cave Collapse — Minute 60).

THE AVENGERS
Stark and Banner suspect SHIELD (who they work for) of wrongdoing (Cave Collapse — Minute 59).

THE HANGOVER
Mike Tyson's friend gives Doug's jacket to Stu (False Light – Minute 59).

A BEAUTIFUL MIND
Parcher refuses to allow John to quit his spying activities (Cave Collapse — Minute 60).

THE CONJURING
Lorraine receives an "insight" to Carolyn's happy family (False Light – Minute 60).

GONE GIRL
Detective Rhonda confirms that Amy was pregnant, much to Nick's shock (Cave Collapse — Minute 60).

THINGS TO KEEP IN MIND FOR ACT 3

Act 3 is what I call "Death Valley." This should be the absolute worst stretch of time in the Main Hero's entire life. You must pound his flaw and his weaknesses over and over until he can no longer take it. It's during this time, around Minute 75, that the Main Hero will experience the lowest point of his existence. Why? As The Mamas & the Papa's used to sing: "The darkest hour is just before dawn."

ACT 3

Death Valley

61

MINUTE 61

PLUS MINUS

A positive turns into a negative, or a negative turns into a positive

The Plus Minus is another way to keep your audience on an emotional roller coaster ride. It's the good-news/bad-news scenario, or vice versa, like in *Raiders of the Last Ark* when Indy is excited about getting the lid open (+), but then he sees the snakes (–); or in *The Godfather* when Michael visits his father in the hospital (+), but discovers there are no guards protecting him (–); and in *Star Wars* when Luke does well with the light saber (+), but then the practice-blaster zaps him (–).

The bodyguard tries to shoot Bond (−) but the gun won't work (+).

Stark tells Banner that his curse of changing into the Hulk (−) might be for a good reason (+).

The tiger that threatens the guys' safety (−) eats the drugged meat (+).

Alicia wants to know if John's okay (+), but he tells her to leave (−).

Demons lurk somewhere in the house (−), but Drew and Andrea connect and smile at each other (+).

Everyone thinks Nick is guilty (−), but Nick gives Margo evidence that he went to a fertility clinic. She believes him (+).

62

MINUTE 62

FLIRTIN' WITH DISASTER

Hero or ally experiences something potentially disastrous

The band Molly Hatchet had a hit with their song, *Flirtin' with Disaster*, which sums up Minute 62 perfectly. Here are a number of ways blockbusters Flirt with Disaster: In *Jaws*, the local girl sees a shark fin in the pond. In *The Matrix*, Neo drinks with Cypher (the man who will betray him). In *Knocked Up*, Debbie thinks Pete is cheating on her.

The guard tells Severine that it's time to cast off — Bond's not coming.

"As soon as Loki took the doctor," says Coulson, "we moved Jane Foster." Thor is relieved to hear this news.

Alan accidentally bangs the tiger's nose into the hallway wall.

John tells Charles that he got himself into something and might need help.

The closet door creaks open.

Margo discovers the letter from Amy's creepy boyfriend.

63

MINUTE 63

ALLY ATTACK

Bad guy, or secondary bad guy, deeply affects hero's ally or love interest

Not only does the bad guy attack the hero, now he takes a swipe at the hero's ally as well. *Will he stop at nothing?* I call this moment Ally Attack. The bad guy who executes this attack can be the out-and-out bad guy, like the shark in *Jaws*, or he can be an ally who's competing for the girl, like Harry in *Spider-Man*. Or he can be a temporary bad guy added during this minute to briefly affect the hero, ally, or love interest, in some way.

SKYFALL

Severine (the Villain's accomplice) has sex with Bond.

A BEAUTIFUL MIND

John sees bad guys enter during his lecture.

THE AVENGERS

Loki's behavior fills Thor with regret.

THE CONJURING

The basement door opens by itself.

THE HANGOVER

The tiger wakes up in the backseat.

GONE GIRL

Nick scrambles to figure out Amy's Clue Three.

64

MINUTE 64

BAD GUY THREAT

Bad Guy, or secondary bad guy, threatens hero in some way

The bad guy keeps up the pressure this minute by posing a threat,
like the enemy ship that fires at the Millennium Falcon in *Star Wars*,
or the Black Panther who threatens Forrest in *Forrest Gump*, or
when Michael Myers grabs Lynda's boyfriend in *Halloween*.

The villain's men kill one of the MI6 agents.

A man in a black hat chases John.

Loki refuses to tell Black Widow what he's done with Agent Barton.

Lorraine feels a threatening presence in the basement.

Mike Tyson's friend growls: "You're late."

Detective Rhonda finds Amy's diary in a furnace.

MINUTE 65

THE RESISTANCE

Hero or ally attacks/resists the bad guy

The bad guys have been putting on the pressure, in some form, the last three minutes. Now it's time for the hero, or his ally, to fight back, like when Indy resists the snakes by torching them in *Raiders of the Lost Ark*, or when Michael resists the enemy by hiding his father in *The Godfather*, or when Forrest tackles the guy who slapped Jenny in *Forrest Gump*.

Bond refuses to leave "before it's too late."

Black Widow manipulates Loki.

Alan pees in Mike Tyson's pool.

John punches the man and runs away.

Ed says to the entity: "Close the door. Move something!"

Nick deciphers Amy's clue and finds the location.

66

MINUTE 66

POSITIVE STEP

Hero does something positive toward his goal

The hero continues his attack, making favorable strides forward on his mission. This is a Positive Step for him, and for the audience. For example: In *Forrest Gump*, Forrest tells Jenny he wants to be her boyfriend. In *The Sixth Sense*, Malcolm studies his old session recordings to find more clues. In *The Godfather*, Michael tells Enzo to stand outside (to help guard his father).

SKYFALL

Bond makes it to the island where the Villain lives.

THE AVENGERS

Captain America searches for the truth.

THE HANGOVER

Stu makes Mike Tyson laugh (he won't kill them now).

A BEAUTIFUL MIND

John goes with the psychologist.

THE CONJURING

In an effort to help the family, Lorraine hangs up their laundry.

GONE GIRL

Amy drives away from Nick.

67

MINUTE 67

HERO EFFECT

Hero does something that will immediately or eventually impact the main bad guy

The hero is on a roll. Let's keep up his momentum during this minute
by showing the hero affecting the main bad guy in some way, like when
Spider-Man blinds Green Goblin and yanks out his flying machine
wires in *Spider-Man*, or when Butch kills his boxing opponent in
Pulp Fiction, which causes Marsellus to lose lots of money.

Bond listens to the Villain/Silva's story, looking for a weakness.

Black Widow draws it out of Loki that he plans on unleashing Banner.

Stu encourages Phil to make a call to Doug's fiancé.

John tries to escape.

Lorraine tells Ed: "You've got to help them."

Amy befriends her pregnant neighbor and "crams her with stories of (her) husband's violent temper."

68

MINUTE 68

ALLY AID

Ally or love interest takes a positive/significant step toward hero

The ally took a beating from the bad guy a few minutes back, but the ally is there for the hero, supposedly, through thick and thin. For example, Han opens the smuggle-door to let Luke and Obi-Wan out in *Star Wars*, and Sgt. Al tries to help John by holding back the police attack in *Die Hard*.

Bond's small GPS in his pocket clues MI6 to his whereabouts.

Stark backs up Captain America in his suspicions about SHIELD.

Phil tells the strangers to take it easy.

Dr. Rosen tells John that Charles is not there.

Carolyn tells Lorraine that she's fine.

The pregnant neighbor asks Amy to use her bathroom (Amy steals her urine).

69

MINUTE 69

CAPTIVATING CONCERN

Something is seen, heard, or experienced that causes great concern

Concern makes its reappearance during Minute 69, but this time with more at stake. In *Knocked Up*, pregnant Alison shows *concern* because Ben wasn't there for her during the earthquake. In *Raiders of the Lost Ark*, Belloq and Marion show *concern* when the Nazi pulls out a torture device. In *Forrest Gump*, Jenny is *concerned* that Forrest doesn't understand that they can't be together.

Silva tells Bond that M lied to him.

Stark is concerned that SHIELD wants to make nuclear weapons.

Stu shows concern for Alan after he's punched.

Alicia is concerned for John's mental health.

Concerned Lorraine watches Carolyn walk away.

Amy cries while writing in her diary.

70

MINUTE 70

NEW JOURNEY

The hero, ally, or bad guy embarks on a new journey

When the characters embark on a New Journey, many questions
are raised that need to be answered: Will they survive it? Will
they be hurt? Will they ultimately succeed? Wanting to know the
answers to these questions keeps us watching, or reading . . .

Silva makes a sexual advance toward Bond.

While The Avengers squabble, Loki's men prepare for attack.

Mr. Chow orders the guys to find his $80,000.

Dr. Rosen tells Alicia that John suffers from paranoia and that Charles never existed.

Ed tells Roger that he was skeptical at first, but he appreciates his help.

Amy cuts her hair and dyes her eyebrows.

71

MINUTE 71

BAD TO THE BONE

Bad guy, or secondary bad guy, shows aggression

Not to be ignored, the bad guy goes on the attack again, in one way or another, for the next seven minutes. He just can't help himself because he's just like that George Thorogood song: *Bad to the Bone.* And he gets badder by the minute . . .

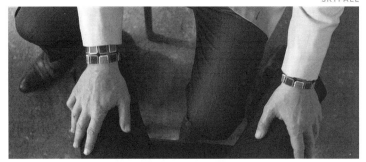

Silva makes an aggressive sexual move on Bond.

Loki's men attack.

Mr. Chow orders the guys to meet him at dawn.

John's paranoia is more obsessive than Alicia thought.

Lorraine saw something horrific during a past exorcism.

Amy devours junk food and soda to change her appearance.

BADDER TO THE BONE

Bad guy, or secondary bad guys, shows more aggression

To keep up the tension, blockbusters show more aggression during this minute in different ways: In *Raiders of the Lost Ark*, Major Toht throws Marion into the snake-filled tomb with Indy. In *The Sixth Sense*, ghosts turn the air cold around frightened Cole. In *Die Hard*, the bad guys shoot out the cops' lights. Here's how our case studies do it:

Silva tells Bond that he could pick his own secret missions, like he does.

Loki's men detonate a bomb.

Phil tells Stu that Melissa "is the worst."

The gate where John delivered the top secret messages was made up in his mind.

Officer Brad hears a voice say: "Look what she made me do."

Amy says: "You think I'd let him destroy me and end up happier than ever? No fucking way."

73

MINUTE 73

BADDEST TO THE BONE

Bad guy, or secondary bad guys, ratchet up aggression even more

Just when you thought the bad guy couldn't get any meaner, he ratchets up his aggression even more. In *Spider-Man*, the Green Goblin knocks out Spidey. In *Raiders of the Lost Ark*, the Nazis seal Indy and Marion inside the tomb. In *Die Hard*, the bad guys shoot two cops.

Silva suggests that he and Bond could control the world.

The enemy's bomb blows up a big chunk of the ship.

Stu's new wife comes back into the picture.

The government official's home John delivered the "top secret messages" to was also part of John's crippling delusion.

A ghost screams at Officer Ed.

Amy strikes herself in the face with a hammer.

74

MINUTE 74

PUT INTO PERIL

Hero and/or ally is put into peril

By this time in the movie, the hero and ally are like our avatars or surrogates for the audience member — an extension of themselves. When the hero and/or ally is Put into Peril, so is the viewer, like when the Green Goblin paralyzes Spider-Man, or when the snakes close in on Indy and Marion in *Raiders of the Lost Ark*, or when Michael is Put into Peril in *The Godfather* by agreeing to kill the police captain.

Severine has been tied up to be executed.

Black Widow is trapped.

The security camera watches Alan win.

John tells Alicia: "They may be listening."

The door slams shut behind Cindy. Ed and Roger can't get into her room.

Nick says: "She's framing me for her murder."

75

MINUTE 75

SKULL AND CROSSBONES

Death or destruction is expressed or threatened

Death comes on strong in these next two minutes, which we'll explore here.
The next two minutes are a heavy reminder that just like in real life, the
things most precious to us — life and love and hopes and dreams — can
be snatched away at any moment, thus the title Skull and Crossbones.

Silva's henchman aims his gun at Bond's head.

John tells Alicia that: "There's a threat that exists of catastrophic proportions."

Loki grins at the destruction he's wrought.

Cindy vanishes with a ghost who said: "Follow me."

Stu reminds Phil and Alan that Doug is still kidnapped and might be killed.

Margo asks Nick: "Does Missouri have the death penalty?"

TURNING POINT 75

Not only are the minutes surrounding Minute 75 occupied by some sort of death (actual death, death of a relationship, etc.), they are also where another major Turning Point happens in the story, usually landing between Minutes 74–76.

More specifically, this Turning Point involves an actual death, a threat of death, or a brief escape from death, as we'll see in our case studies below:

SKYFALL

Silva and his thugs force Bond outside to shoot the girl (Minute 75) — *threat of death.*

THE AVENGERS

Bruce Banner turns into the Hulk (Minute 75) — *threat of death.*

THE HANGOVER

Alan begins winning an insane amount of money at the table. The guys might be able to pay Doug's ransom (Minute 75) — *narrowly avoiding Doug's death.*

A BEAUTIFUL MIND

Alicia shows John that the secret packages he dropped off for the government to pick up were never opened. "There is no conspiracy," she tells him (Minute 76) — *death of his illusion that the government is out to kill him.*

THE CONJURING

The entity takes Cindy (Minute 75) – *threat of death.*

GONE GIRL

Nick learns that Missouri has the death penalty (Minute 75) — *threat of death.*

76

MINUTE 76

DEATH TAP

Death or destruction, or their threat, is escalated

And as the hero walks deeper into the Valley of Death — as referred to in King David's Old Testament verse, "Yea though I walk through the valley of the shadow of death" — the black-hooded Grim Reaper, in some way, taps him on the shoulder with the tip of his scythe. Here are a few ways he does it during Minute 76:

Silva kills Severine.

The enemy has destroyed a main part of the ship.

Mr. Chow waits for the guys and his money.

The nurse says into the phone: "Dr. Rosen, Code Red."

Cindy says, "That's where Rory hides when he's afraid."

Amy uses the Internet to assure that Nick gets the death penalty.

77

MINUTE 77

THE RUMBLE

A fight, argument, or violent act occurs

The tension of death needs a release, and this is the minute where that happens. The release comes in the form of a fight. It's time to rumble, either physically or emotionally. Whichever one you choose, a fight breaks out either way . . .

Bond fights Silva's henchmen.

Thor fights the Hulk.

The guys argue whether they should flick the lights or not.

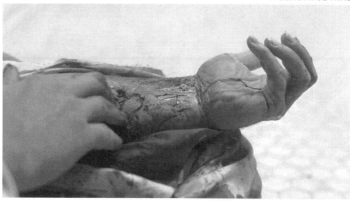

John tears open his skin, looking for the implant.

The house pulls Lorraine downward as she fights against it.

Amy's new neighbor argues with her boyfriend.

78

MINUTE 78

MYSTERY MISSION

Hero and ally interact; there's a mystery that needs to be solved

Okay, death has made an appearance and it caused a fight, but now the screenwriter must plant something during the next couple of minutes to keep the viewer watching. What they do is create a Mystery Mission. Mystery creates curiosity and spurs *more* questions. That curiosity *has* to be satisfied. Those questions *have* to be answered.

Bond glances at M, wondering what she will say to Silva.

Captain America asks Stark what their next move is.

Mr. Chow's guy yanks a man with a sack over his head out of the car.

Alicia watches John being strapped onto a gurney. John wonders what's going to happen to him.

Ed listens for Lorraine in the walls. Where did she fall?

Amy and her new neighbor chat. Amy refuses to tell her what really happened to her face.

79

MINUTE 79

MYSTERY MISSION 2

Hero and/or ally continue to engage/interact; more mystery

Mystery Mission 2 prompts the curious hero or the audience to continue asking questions. In *Top Gun,* we wonder what the mysterious classified information contains. In *The Sixth Sense,* we wonder what's in the box. When Dewey and Gale find Neil Prescott's car in *Scream,* they wonder aloud: "What's he doing here?"

M engages with Silva who keeps his real plan a mystery. *What's he planning to do?*

Fury tells Agent Hill: "We need full evac on the lower hangar bay." *Will that be enough to repel the enemy?*

The hooded man is not their friend Doug. *Where's Doug?*

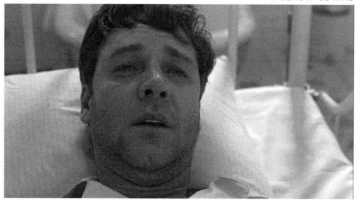

John looks at Alicia — *What's happening to me?*

Lorraine hears someone speaking. *Who is that? Where's that noise coming from?*

Amy and her new neighbor continue to chat. Amy tells her some things, but not all. The neighbor wonders: *What's she hiding?*

80

MINUTE 80

TICK TICK BOOM

An emotional or physical explosion occurs

Just like a stick of dynamite with a timer attached, the tension has built since Minute 70's New Journey began, which has taken the hero through the Valley Of Death, a fight, and a couple unanswered questions. The frustration and stress is too much and the dynamite has finally ignited. As a result, an explosion surprises the hero or ally. Sometimes it's an actual explosion. Most of the time, though, it's an emotional explosion.

Silva springs to his feet and demands that M say his real name.

The enemy fires at furious Hulk.

Phil screams: "Goddammit!"

John writhes because of the electric shock.

A hanging woman drops. Lorraine screams!

Attorney Tanner Bolt bursts out laughing at Nick's story.

81

MINUTE 81

SURPRISED HERO

Bad guy or ally surprises hero

Not only does the explosion surprise the hero or ally, the surprises keep coming over the next two minutes. If your hero is surprised, your audience will be too. Here's how our case studies surprise the hero:

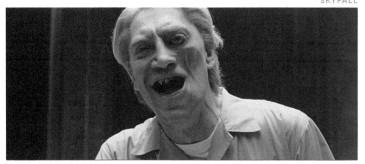

Silva pulls out his retainer. Bond sees Silva's disfigured face.

Enemy soldiers surprise Captain America.

Drug-dealer Doug's enlightening roofies comment surprises Stu.

Sol surprises Alicia by asking how she's doing through all this.

A demonic spirit lifts Nancy and propels her.

Tanner Bolt finds a witness against Nick's wife with amazing speed, which impresses Nick.

82

MINUTE 82

SURPRISE-SURPRISE

Another quick surprise happens

I once visited Dracula's Castle in Wildwood, New Jersey — a boardwalk horror
funhouse teenage friends and I were curious about. As we felt our way through
the dark hallways, passing tableaux of dungeon scenes and guillotines, an
occasional funhouse employee, costumed as a demon or ghoul, would dart out
at us. Toward the end of the twelve-minute tour, however, they hit us with two
surprises in a row: A hissing vampire leapt out of a concealed compartment
and a werewolf barked out a blood-curdling howl above us. The vampire
startled me, yes, but the werewolf *really* surprised me. That's what Minute 82's
Surprise-Surprise is about: to follow up with another unexpected scare.

Imprisoned Silva laughs when Bond and M leave.

Hawkeye surprises Fury.

Stu tackles Phil.

Sol pays John a surprise visit.

Lorraine sees the dead body of her daughter floating in the water.

Amy's ex-boyfriend tells Nick that Amy falsely accused him of rape.

83

MINUTE 83

GOTTA GO!

Hero hurries somewhere

If we were strolling through the city and we saw someone sprinting down the sidewalk, we would stop for a few moments and watch, wouldn't we? What are they running away from? What are they hurrying toward? The screenwriter uses this same Gotta Go! technique to hold the audience's attention.

Q hurries to break Silva's encryption.

Iron Man hurries to restore the propeller.

The guys hurry back to the hotel to look for Doug.

John hurriedly changes the subject as to why Bender didn't visit him.

Ed and Lorraine hurry to get the priest.

Amy's ex-boyfriend tells Nick how he hurried into a relationship with Amy because she was beautiful and smart.

GAP SUBTRACT

Gap between hero and bad guy/ally decreases

If someone steps into our personal space, we have no choice but to pay attention. I call this the Gap Subtract. It forces the hero to react. It works the same way for the audience during Minute 84, like in *Top Gun* when the MiGs close in on Maverick, or in *Raiders of the Lost Ark* when Indy closes in on the Nazi trucks, or in *Jaws* when the shark swims closer to the boat.

SKYFALL

Bond says to Q: "Stop, go in on that (Silva's cryptic code on the screen). Q brings the numbers closer to Bond.

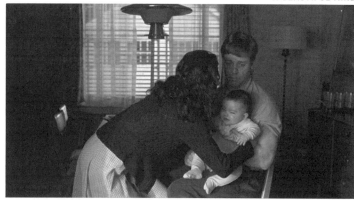

A BEAUTIFUL MIND

Alicia comes to take the crying baby from John.

THE AVENGERS

Thor approaches Loki.

THE CONJURING

Ed and Lorraine show Father Gordon their footage in hopes of getting an exorcism.

THE HANGOVER

Doug tackles Phil.

GONE GIRL

Nick and Amy's ex-boyfriend share similar stories.

85

MINUTE 85

BAD GUY BOO-BOO

Bad guy is hurt

I call this minute Bad Guy Boo-Boo, referring to what my friend's mom used to call scrapes on the knee or accidental burns. This is the minute we see hints that the bad guy is vulnerable. There's a chink in his armor. He has an Achilles' heel. When the audience sees this weakness, they'll think it just might be possible for the hero to defeat him. The audience will stick around to see if it actually happens.

Bond figures out Silva's key.

Black Widow hurts Loki-controlled Hawkeye.

Stu hurts the stripper's feelings.

John has his paranoia under control.

Father Gordon says he will push Ed and Lorraine's exorcism request through to the Vatican himself.

Amy's new neighbor says that Amy (on the TV news) was an uppity rich bitch, which Amy hates.

ACT 3
CHECKLIST

- Have you kept your dialogue and scenes centered around the theme?
- Have you made the Main Hero go through the absolute worst experiences of his life?
- Is there tension and conflict in every scene, and in every bit of dialogue?
- Is the Main Hero fully aware of his flaw now? Does he see how his flaw has been a major hindrance in his life?

THE FINAL
QUEST

This is when the Main Hero heads toward his final battle with the Villain, which usually happens between Minutes 85–100. This is the act where (for a happy ending) the Main Hero will sacrifice his flaw for the greater good, defeat the Villain, and be rewarded; or (for a tragic ending) the Main Hero will refuse to give up his flaw and do the greater good. As a result, he suffers and is not rewarded (but we still learn from his mistake).

SKYFALL'S FINAL QUEST
Bond tells M that it's time to "get out in front; change the game." He heads toward Skyfall where his final battle against Silva will happen. (Minute 99)

THE AVENGERS' FINAL QUEST
Captain America tells Black Widow, "Time to go." — They're heading to Stark's building where Loki will be. (Minute 97)

THE HANGOVER'S FINAL QUEST
The guys race back to Doug's father-in-law's place — to try to make it on time for the wedding. (Minute 87)

A BEAUTIFUL MIND'S FINAL QUEST
John refuses to take meds — he's going to try to ignore his imaginary friends and be a normal working person again. (Minute 99)

THE CONJURING'S FINAL QUEST
Lorraine says to Ed: "Let's finish this together." (Minute 90)

GONE GIRL'S FINAL QUEST
Nick and Tanner Bolt prepare to go on nationwide TV to discuss Nick's infidelity. (Minute 97)

ACT 4

The Final Quest

(Starts between Minutes 85 and 100, depending on your story.)

86

MINUTE 86

WORRY WOUND

Hero or ally is wounded in some way

Something happens during Minute 86 that worries one of our main characters
and wounds him. And when a Worry Wound occurs, it has to be remedied
in some way, like in *The Matrix* when Cypher shoots Tank and Dozer.

Bond sees that Silva has escaped.

Thor can't get out of the falling pod.

Stu learns he pulled out his own tooth.

John sees that Alicia thinks he's relapsed into talking to himself.

Ed and Lorraine's daughter enters the forbidden room.

Nick tells Margo that Tanner Bolt's retainer is $100,000, way more than Nick has.

87

MINUTE 87

DAMAGE DONE

Bad guy provokes physical or emotional damage

The bad guy may have been hurt a couple minutes ago, but this only made him angrier. He's going to retaliate here until there's Damage Done, especially during the next two minutes . . .

Bond sees a train coming.

The enemy soldier's bullets pin down Captain America.

Tracy's pout hurts her worried father.

John is unable to have sex with Alicia.

A demonic spirit pounds on Ed and Lorraine's daughter's door.

TV host suggests that Nick and his sister are lovers.

88

MINUTE 88

DOUBLE DAMAGE DONE

Bad guy causes additional physical or emotional damage

The villain continues to cause damage during this minute, like in *Raiders of the Lost Ark* when the German soldier punches Indy's wounded arm and throws him through the windshield, or in *Scream* when the killer stabs Dewey and then chases Sidney, or in *Knocked Up* when the bouncer tells pregnant Alison she's a bad parent.

The train almost kills Bond.

Worried Fury speaks to dying Coulson, who Loki stabbed.

Tracy looks for Doug.

John's lack of sexual interest makes Alicia scream and break the glass cup.

The Annabelle doll scares Ed and Lorraine's daughter. She screams!

Amy tells police about "strange activity" near Margo's woodshed.

89

MINUTE 89

RED ALERT!

Circumstances grow more serious for hero

We've all seen that moment in WWII movies where the aircraft carrier's speakers blare out *Red Alert! Red Alert!* as the enemy's torpedo races toward the crippled and vulnerable hull. In a sense, this is what's happening to the hero during this minute . . .

Bond can't find Silva in the train.

Fury tosses Coulson's bloody cards at Captain America and says: "We're dead in the air."

The guys are running extremely late for the wedding. They dress on the way there.

An emotional distance grows between Alicia and John.

The demonic spirit throws a chair at Ed, Lorraine, and their daughter.

Mr. Collings, Amy's creepy ex, refuses to help Nick.

90

MINUTE 90

RESCUING ALLY

Ally helps the hero

And just when things have gone *Red Alert* for the hero, the ally comes to the rescue! In *Raiders of the Lost Ark*, Sallah helps Indy and Marion escape. In *Knocked Up,* Debbie tells pregnant and miserable Alison she's young and beautiful. Let's see how the ally comes to the rescue in our case studies:

Q tells Bond to get on the train.

Fury tries to inspire the discouraged Avengers.

Tracy's father winks at Doug and whispers, "Vegas."

Alicia gives John his pills.

Lorraine says: "Let's finish this together."

Tanner Bolt shows up in Missouri to help Nick.

TURNING POINT 90

If your story is to continue on, another major Turning Point must happen at this point to keep the audience disoriented and guessing. Most times you do this by adding a big complication for the hero that's going to take some time to solve, as in *Skyfall, The Avengers, A Beautiful Mind*, and *The Conjuring*. Or you bring in a surprise guest who will help the hero solve his big problem, as in *Gone Girl*. This Turning Point usually occurs between Minutes 89–91.

SKYFALL
Bond learns that Silva is headed toward the courthouse to kill M. (Minute 91)

THE AVENGERS
Thor is unable to lift his hammer. (Minute 91)

A BEAUTIFUL MIND
John has secretly stopped taking his medication. (Minute 90)

THE CONJURING
Possessed Carolyn drives her daughter back toward the evil house. (Minute 90)

GONE GIRL
Tanner Bolt arrives in Missouri to help Nick avoid the death penalty. (Minute 90)

91

MINUTE 91

SUFFER THE WEAK

Hero or ally expresses weakness

When we see someone we care about suffering, or they are brave
enough to tell you their weakness, we pity or sympathize with them.
We've all had those moments of suffering and weakness and can relate.
So it is with the characters we've been watching on the screen . . .

Scared M learns Silva has escaped.

Thor can't pick up his hammer.

Melissa yanks open Stu's mouth. Stu says: "Ow."

John's paranoia returns because he hasn't been taking his pills.

Ed tells Lorraine: "I can't lose you."

Nick tells Tanner Bolt: "She's taking me on a tour of my infidelities, rubbing my nose in it."

92

MINUTE 92

HUGS AND KISSES

Hero and ally/love interest show affection

The hero and ally have been through hell the last fifteen minutes, and as a result they've grown closer and will show affection toward each other in the next two minutes. Here's how our case studies hug and kiss during Minute 92:

Tanner supports M during the Prime Minister's attack.

Black Widow tells Hawkeye: "You're going to be alright."

Stu and Alan join forces against Melissa.

John tells Parcher that Dr. Rosen said he (Parcher) is not real.

Lorraine reaches out her arms to help Roger's daughter.

Nick and Tanner Bolt help each other build a case against Amy.

93

MINUTE 93

HUGS AND KISSES 2

Hero and ally express even greater affection

The hero and ally continue their affection toward each other during Minute 93, like when Quint, Brody, and Hooper laugh and sing together in *Jaws*, or when Maverick says he's "not leaving without my wingman" in *Top Gun*, or in *The Sixth Sense* when Malcolm sits beside the sleeping Anna and talks lovingly to her.

Mallory sticks up for M.

Hawkeye thanks Black Widow.

Stu and the guys do a group hug.

John tells Alicia that he'll draw the baby's bath, which makes her smile.

Lorraine, Ed, and Roger try to help Carolyn.

Nick and Tanner Bolt discuss protecting Margo the accomplice.

94

MINUTE 94

THE AGGRESSOR

Hero or bad guy shows aggression

As mentioned earlier, we gave the hero and the ally — and the audience — an emotional breather for a couple minutes. But now the action kicks in again as the bad guy shows aggression . . .

Silva blows out the wall behind Bond.

Alicia sees that John's paranoia has returned.

Hawkeye says: "If I put an arrow in Loki's eye socket I'd feel better."

Lorraine yells at Ed: "I'm not leaving!"

Phil gives Doug's marriage "six months." Stu calls Phil a dick. **The End**

Amy says: "I'm not the asshole," and strikes the ball hard.

THE SEPARATION

Hero and ally separate

The Separation is another trick writers have up their coffee-stained sleeves. Separation creates a longing because we immediately desire for the separated parties to be reunited. It's an unresolved issue that must be followed up on somehow. Here's how our case studies create separations, either physically or emotionally:

Silva climbs the ladder away from Bond.

Black Widow wants to fight Loki, but Hawkeye doesn't want her to be part of a war.

Alicia runs from John.

Lorraine leaves Ed to get the book.

Amy's new neighbor (now the aggressor) teases Amy and heads back to her cabin.

96

MINUTE 96

DEATH AND DYING

Some kind of death is shown or expressed

Showing or speaking about death always grabs attention, that's why it's used a few times during a movie. Death and Dying are primal. Death threatens our very existence. Death supercharges our fight or flight response . . .

Silva's men kill the security guards.

Stark and Captain America talk about Coulson's death.

Parcher tells John that countless people will die.

Crows slam into the house.

Tanner Bolt tells Margo: "(Nick will be) a trained monkey who doesn't get a *lethal injection*."

97

MINUTE 97

TAPING THE KNUCKLES

Hero prepares for, or heads toward, the battle place

Football players strap on their helmets . . . boxers tape their knuckles . . . soldiers load their rifles as they prep for the battle place. Anticipation fills the air as the hero prepares himself for the Big Showdown . . .

SKYFALL

Bond runs toward Silva.

A BEAUTIFUL MIND

John battles his imaginary friends.

THE AVENGERS

Captain America tells Black Widow: "Time to go." — They're heading to Stark's building where Loki will be.

THE CONJURING

Ed asks everyone to hold Carolyn still.

GONE GIRL

Nick and Tanner Bolt prepare to go on nationwide TV to discuss Nick's infidelity.

98

MINUTE 98

KISS OR SPIT

Hero or bad guy shows aggression/affection

The story can go two different ways in the next three minutes. If the movie is ending here on an upbeat note, the hero shows affection (kiss). If not, aggression is shown (spits), which continues the story in most cases.

Silva shoots at M (Spits).

Captain America marches toward the plane, ready to fight (Spits).

John prevents Alicia from driving (Spits).

The demon shrieks at Ed (Spits).

Amy's new neighbors force their way into her cabin (Spits).

KISS OR SPIT 2

Hero or bad guy shows even more aggression/affection

The hero or villain kiss or spit even more during this minute, like when the Green Goblin drops Mary Jane (Spit), or in *Raiders of the Lost Ark* when Indy beats up a German soldier and steals his clothes (Spit), or when Forrest shows affection toward Bubba's mother by giving her money in *Forrest Gump* (Kiss).

Bond tells M (in the back seat) that it's time to "get out in front; change the game." (Kiss)

Iron Man orders the doctor to shut his deadly machine down (Spits).

John refuses to take meds again (Spits).

The demon turns Carolyn upside-down (Spits).

Amy's neighbor attacks her (Spits).

KISS OR SPIT 3

Hero and/or bad guy show even greater aggression/affection

And the kissing and spitting continues for another minute. In *The Matrix*, Neo and Trinity shoot the security guards (Spit). In *Pulp Fiction*, Butch knocks out The Gimp (Spit). In *Top Gun*, the Chief shakes Maverick's hand and smiles (Kiss).

Bond orders M to get in (Spits/Kiss).

Loki tells Stark that his army is coming (Spits).

John yells at Dr. Rosen (Spits).

The demon tells Roger that Carolyn is "already gone." (Spits)

Amy's new neighbors steal her money (Spits).

101

MINUTE 101

DEEPER DEEPER

Hero heads deeper into trouble

The deeper the hero goes, the deeper into trouble he gets. The deeper into trouble he gets, the more the audience gnaws on their nails, wanting to see how he'll get out of it, like in *Raiders of the Lost Ark* when Indy follows the Nazis deeper into the mountains, or in *Jaws* when the shark pulls the crew further out to sea.

SKYFALL

M asks: "Where are we going?" "Back in time," Bond responds.

THE AVENGERS

Stark tells Loki: "There's no version of this where you come out on top."

A BEAUTIFUL MIND

John tells Alicia: "I will try to figure this out."

THE CONJURING

Ed climbs deeper into the house after Carolyn.

GONE GIRL

Nick rehearses in St. Louis for his nationwide TV interview.

102

MINUTE 102

THE BLOW-UP

There's an emotional or physical blow-up

And there's bound to be a Blow-Up the deeper into enemy territory the hero goes. The villain feels threatened and retaliates. It's inevitable. Nothing like a physical or emotional *blast* to jar the audience, which is Minute 102's purpose . . .

Mallory walks in on Q and Tanner breaking MI6 rules.

Iron Man's beam strikes Loki.

John's life and family have been destroyed because of his illness.

Carolyn violently throws up.

Amy calls her creepy ex-boyfriend for help.

103

MINUTE 103

THE BLOW

Hero or bad guy administers some sort of blow

Another Blow follows the previous minute's blast. The one-two punch, as it were. Again, this can be a physical blow or an emotional blow, as we see in *Spider-Man* when the Green Goblin strikes Spidey hard with his foot, or when Han says he's not going to help the cause (an emotional blow to Luke) in *Star Wars*.

"How old were you when they died?" M asks. "You know the answer to that,"
Bond replies coldly.

Iron Man blows up the approaching enemy.

John doesn't know what else to do.

Ed and Lorraine defeat the demon and restore Roger and Carolyn's family.

Nick's college girlfriend makes a nationwide TV statement about her affair
with Nick.

104

MINUTE 104

THE UPPER HAND

Hero or bad guy gets the upper hand in an aggressive manner

The phrase "The Upper Hand" evolved when kids gathered to pick sides for sandlot baseball games. To decide who chooses first, one team captain would toss the other captain a baseball bat. The two captains then took turns gripping the bat one fist over the other until there was no more room at the top. The last one to fully grip the bat's handle had control, or "The Upper Hand." The hero and the bad guy play this same game, but for much higher stakes during this minute.

Bond forces M to go with him to Skyfall.

Loki's beam strikes Thor.

Alicia tells John: "I need to believe that something extraordinary is possible."

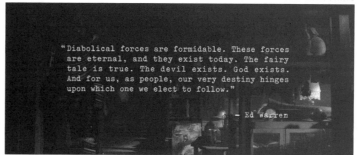

Ed tells the doubters in the final title: "The fairy tale is true. The devil exists."
The End

Amy's mother decries Nick on nationwide TV.

105

MINUTE 105

THE DECEIT

Deceit is shown or expressed

Deceit works well three ways. If it is against the hero, we hold our breath and anticipate what's going to happen next; if it's against the bad guy, we cheer; if it's against us, the audience, we silently applaud the storyteller for getting one over on us . . .

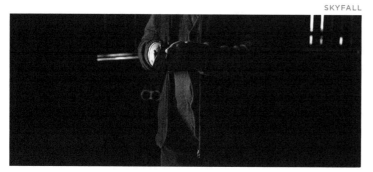

Someone's been hiding in the house.

John shows up unannounced at Hansen's office.

Thor tackles Loki — he wasn't as wounded as he appeared to be.

Nick stares at the interviewer, acting calm and collected.

TURNING POINT 105

If your story is continuing, another major Turning Point happens between Minutes 104–106. In fact, as I mentioned in this book's opening pages, if you want to expand your story indefinitely, simply add a big Turning Point every fifteen minutes — a Turning Point that will take some doing for the hero to unravel or resolve. This is a longtime secret trick writers use to extend any story, a trick you can use at Minute 120 to keep the story going if the story requires it, and again at Minutes 135 and 150 and so on . . .

SKYFALL
Bond discovers that Kincade, the groundskeeper, still works at Skyfall. He can help them fight Silva. (Minute 105)

THE AVENGERS
Black Widow tricks Loki into revealing that he plans on unleashing the Hulk. (Minute 105)

A BEAUTIFUL MIND
John heads back to campus to try to regain his life. He asks Hansen for a teaching job. (Minute 105)

GONE GIRL
Nick's young mistress publicly confesses about her and Nick's affair, just before his big TV interview. (Minute 104)

106

MINUTE 106

THE DODGE

Someone dodges or avoids something

When the hero or ally has to dodge or avoid something bad, we wince for them. It makes us almost want to scream: "Watch out!" (I've actually heard people scream *look out* during The Dodge while watching action movies in theaters.) Their dilemma keeps us emotionally invested.

SKYFALL

Bond thought there were no weapons in the house, but Kincade saved James's father's old hunting rifle (barely dodges being weaponless).

THE AVENGERS

Hawkeye's plane *barely* avoids hitting pedestrians.

A BEAUTIFUL MIND

Hansen says: "I wanted to write . . ." (dodges the fact that he hasn't contacted John).

GONE GIRL

Nick did great in the interview (he dodged a media bullet).

MINUTE 107

GOOD DOES BAD

Someone that seems good does bad

Pro screenwriters design Minute 107 to give the audience a glimpse into the hero or ally's darker side — by showing us that good can indeed do bad. Why? The audience needs to know that the hero and his friends have what it takes to fight — and possibly defeat — the villain in the final brutal battle.

Kincade tells Bond: "Try to stop me, you jumped-up little shit."

Loki seemed to soften and connect with his brother, but then he stabs him.

John slams the newspaper when Charles appears.

Amy's ex-boyfriend, who's helping her, shuts off the TV so she can't watch news.

108

MINUTE 108

SENSE OF FINALITY

Finality is shown or expressed

The Sense of Finality during Minute 108 is used for two reasons:
Either to help wrap up the story or a subplot, or to create a sense
of impending doom to propel the movie forward . . .

Kincade tells M that when James came out of the hiding spot after his parents died, he wasn't a boy anymore.

Captain America says: "They're fish in a barrel down there."

John tells Hansen: "I am quite certain you will say no."

Amy's creepy ex-boyfriend says: "I am not letting you get away again."

109

MINUTE 109

THE EXTRAORDINARY

Something extraordinary is revealed

Since there was a false sense of finality in the last minute, the writer jump-starts the story again by revealing something extraordinary. This always causes a bigger question to be raised. And when a bigger question is raised, it needs to be answered somehow, like in *Die Hard* when John discovers an extraordinary amount of explosives near the roof.

Aged M knows how to effortlessly make explosives.

Hawkeye tells Black Widow: "You and I remember Budapest way differently."

The librarian says John is "going nuts."

Amy's creepy ex says he wants her to look like she used to.

110

MINUTE 110

STRONG STATEMENT

Someone makes a strong statement, either verbally or physically

A Strong Statement is made either visually or, most of the time, verbally during this minute. Again, this statement is designed to propel the story forward and get the hero deeper into trouble. In *Spider-Man*, Mary Jane tells Peter she loves him. In *The Matrix*, Tank says that Neo is "The One." In *Pulp Fiction*, Jules says: "I will strike down upon thee with great vengeance."

Kincade blows a hole through the door with a sawed-off shotgun.

Captain America proves to the cop why he should take orders from him.

John tells Alicia: "Maybe Rosen's right. Maybe I ought to think about going back into the hospital again."

Amy's creepy ex says: "I am looking forward to my reunion with Amy Elliot."

MINUTE 111

TURN FOR THE WORSE

Things take a turn for the worse for the hero

Another great way to grab the audience's attention, or to extend the story if you need to, is to have the movie take a Turn for the Worse. It's a problem that has to be solved, which keeps the audience watching until it's *re*solved, like in *The Matrix* when the agents order sentinels to destroy the Nebuchadnezzar.

Silva's henchmen arrive.

Charles stands in John's way.

Banner tells The Avengers: "So, this all seems horrible."

The TV interviewer tells Nick: ". . . we know you're a liar."

MINUTE 112

CHARGING SHARK

Bad guy takes aggressive action toward hero and ally

From Minute 112 to the end of the movie, the bad guy comes on strong in the form of aggressive action, or as I prefer to call it: Charging Shark (referring to the shark that rushes toward Hooper in *Jaws*). We're gonna go through these remaining minutes pretty quickly, so stay focused . . .

SKYFALL

Silva's henchman presses an explosive on the door.

A BEAUTIFUL MIND

Parcher glares at John.

THE AVENGERS

The enemy ship rushes toward Banner.

GONE GIRL

The TV interviewer says to Nick sarcastically: "You talk like you want to make amends with your wife."

THE CAGE SLAM

Bad guy takes another aggressive action toward hero and allies

The Cage Slam refers to the moment the shark rams into
Hooper's fragile cage during this minute in *Jaws*. Here are other
ways our case studies rattle our hero and ally's cages:

The henchmen shoot at Bond.

Charles tells John that he's being pathetic.

Loki says: "Send the rest."

The TV interviewer says to Nick: "Look at the lens and talk to your wife."

GETS THE BETTER

Bad guy gets the better of hero and/or ally

We think the hero might have a chance, but then the bad guy Gets the Better of him, which increases the audience's anxiety, like when Agent Smith Gets the Better of Neo in *The Matrix*, or when the Death Star blasts away at Luke in *Star Wars*.

Silva arrives in an attack helicopter.

Hawkeye says: "Stark, you have a lot of strays sniffing your tail."

Parcher lets John know he's still watching him.

Detective Rhonda brings a search warrant and opens the woodshed.

MINUTE 115

BLEAK MEEK

Things seem bleak for the hero

It looks like the suddenly passive hero (meek) might be defeated after all (bleak). In *Die Hard*, John runs from the FBI's bullets (meek) before they can kill him (bleak). In *Jaws*, defeated Quint and Brody (meek) pull up the mutilated cage — Hooper's not in it (bleak).

Silva's helicopter unloads on Bond (bleak). He hides to avoid the bullets (meek).

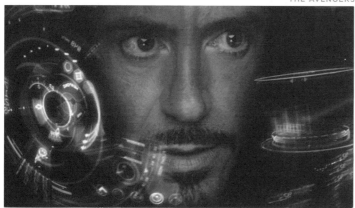

While being chased by the enemy, Stark sees his only option is a narrow tunnel (bleak). Caught between a rock and a hard place, he says: "Oh boy" (meek).

John's imaginary friend gestures for a hug (bleak). He ignores her (meek).

Nick watches his sister (meek) being arrested (bleak).

KICK 'EM WHILE THEY'RE DOWN

Bad guy exerts tremendous effort against hero

The bad guy sees that the hero is hurt, so he's going to Kick 'Em While He's Down to make sure he doesn't rise back up. In *Jaws,* the shark leaps onto the boat to attack Brody. In *The Matrix*, Agent Smith punches Neo's stomach with incredible speed. In *Pulp Fiction*, Jimmy yells at Jules for bringing a dead girl to his house.

Silva's helicopters fire the big guns at the house.

A student (former bad guy in John's past) wants John to look at his theory.

An enemy soldier tackles Black Widow.

Amy's creepy ex says he's moving in with her. "I just want you to be you again."

MINUTE 117

THE REPRIEVE

Looks really, really bleak for hero, but hero does something that might save him

You may find the phrase *"Yes, but…"* helpful when writing this minute.
Yes, it does look really bad for the hero during this minute, *but* he
does something that might give him a glimmer of hope . . .

Yes Silva throws bombs, *but* Bond finds an automatic rifle.

Yes the enemy's attack intensifies, *but* Thor and Hulk help each other.

Yes John is surrounded by students (who he used to hate), *but* now he teaches them.

Yes Nick is in trouble, *but* he tells Tanner Bolt: "The truth is my defense."

HOPE MIGHT BE LOST

Hope might be lost for good for the hero

Nope, forget that glimmer of hope in the last minute. Hope Might
Be Lost for good during Minute 118 as the bad guy hurts the hero,
or ally, even more, like in *Jaws* when the boat sinks as the shark
closes in on Brody, or when Sonny is killed in *The Godfather*.

M is severely wounded.

The enemy is going to kill a lot of civilians.

John says that he'd like to teach, but Hansen replies: "A classroom of fifty would be daunting for anyone" (suggesting John may not be able to handle it).

Nick is arrested for murder.

ONE BULLET LEFT

Hero fails, or needs help, as the bad guy closes in

It's never easy, is it? So it is for our hero, who goes to meet the bad guy with only One Bullet Left in his chamber, either literally or figuratively. In *Jaws*, Brody shoots but fails to hit the air canister. In *The Godfather*, Tom needs a drink to gain the courage to tell Don Corleone that his son is dead. In *Forrest Gump*, guilt overcomes Forrest when Jenny tells him he's her son's father.

Silva firebombs Skyfall with Bond still inside, running out of ammo.

Captain America can't break free from the enemy soldier.

John asks a student if she can see that man talking to him. She says yes.

Amy turns the tables — she kisses her creepy ex and musses his hair.

POWDER KEG

There's an emotional or physical explosion

Minute 120 is the Powder Keg that will, or finally does, blow. And it comes in the form of a physical or emotional explosion. And this explosion is much more intense than the previous explosions. In *Knocked Up*, Alison screams in pain. In *Die Hard*, Argyle crashes into the bad guy's van. In *The Godfather*, Don Corleone bursts into tears over his son's death. In *Jaws*, the shark explodes!

Bond's car explodes!

Hawkeye's arrow blows up in Loki's hand!

John is told that he's being considered for the Nobel Prize!

Amy slams herself against the door and screams!

ACT 4
CHECKLIST

- Have you kept your dialogue and scenes centered around your theme?
- Did your Main Hero head toward the final battle place and defeat the Villain?
- Did your Main Hero sacrifice his flaw for the greater good?
- Did the Main Hero suffer for sacrificing his flaw?

- Did you reward your hero for sacrificing his flaw and defeating the Villain?
- If your story is a tragedy, did the Main Hero fail to give up his flaw and do the greater good? Did we learn something from his failings?

WHAT IF MY
SCREENPLAY IS
LONGER THAN
120 PAGES?

If, after numerous and painstaking rewrites, you still feel like you need more than 120 pages to tell your story, then you'll need to add a new Act — Act 5. You'll have to bump up the moment when the Main Hero sacrifices his flaw for the greater good, and include it here. This is also where the Main Hero will: suffer for giving up his flaw, defeat the Villain, and be rewarded for his sacrifices (happy ending); or he fails to give up his flaw, but we still learn a lesson from his failings (tragedy).

Here's how our Main Heroes sacrificed their flaws for the greater good, suffered for it, then were rewarded:

HAPPY ENDINGS

Skyfall: Overcoming his age and disappointments in M (*flaw*), Bond shoots the ice below his feet to give M better odds to live (*sacrifices himself for the greater good*). He almost drowns in the process (*suffers*). In the end, Eve gives Bond a gift from M: her desk bulldog. Bond smiles (*reward*).

The Avengers: Overcoming his selfishness (*flaw*), Tony Stark intercepts the missile and carries it through the wormhole toward the Chitauri fleet — a suicide mission. The missile destroys the Chitauri mother ship (*sacrifices for the greater good*). Despite the Hulk's help, Stark crashes to the ground, which hurts him badly (*suffers*). His selfless act earns the respect of Captain America who previously disrespected Stark (*reward*).

The Hangover: Overcoming his blind love for mean Melissa (*flaw*), Stu breaks up with Melissa at Doug's wedding, much to everyone's relief (*sacrifices for the greater good*). She pokes Stu and yells at him in front of everyone (*suffers*). The guys give Stu a group hug (*reward*).

A Beautiful Mind: Overcoming his social awkwardness and feelings of intellectual superiority (*flaw*), John begins teaching students out of the goodness of his heart (*sacrifices for the greater good*). His imaginary friends continue to stalk him (*suffers*), but John ignores them. In the end John earns the respect of his wife and colleagues and wins the Nobel Prize (*reward*).

The Conjuring: Overcoming her fear of demons (*flaw*), Lorraine stays in the haunted house to cast the demon out of Carolyn (*sacrifices for the greater good*). Afterwards, she walks out of the house, exhausted (*suffers*). Carolyn's daughter gives Lorraine her lost necklace back (*reward*).

TRAGIC ENDING

Gone Girl: Failing to overcome his need to please everyone (*flaw*), Nick takes psychopathic Amy back (*fails to sacrifice for the greater good*) to please the media. He now has to live with her and raise her child (*suffers*). He's given no reward. We learn that *trying to please everyone leads to misery*.

I appreciate you taking time to read my book. You now have screenwriting secrets of successful movies at the ready.

People say that "knowledge is power" — and, hopefully, you've gained many insights from *Beat by Beat* — but I've come to learn from working in entertainment that knowledge without action and hard work is power*less*. You must be willing to rewrite your scripts numerous times until each scene and act finds its sweet spot. In 1958 Ernest Hemingway told *The Paris Review* that he rewrote the ending to *A Farewell To Arms* thirty-nine times. And therein lies the secret to his success, and the success of the screenwriters who wrote the films you just studied in this book: They not only learned the technical aspects of storytelling, but it was their willingness to spend endless hours refining characters, themes, arcs, and dialogue to perfection that gave their tales a fighting chance at greatness.

This kind of greatness is available to you, too.

If you'd like to see more minute-by-minute story beats, which include forty successful movies like *Star Wars, The Matrix, Raiders of the Lost Ark,* and other classics, check out my bestseller *Something Startling Happens: The 120 Story Beats Every Writer Needs to Know.* You can find it at mwp.com. Or check out my treatment-writing e-book *The Screenwriter's Fairy Tale* on Amazon.

All the best,
Todd Klick. Los Angeles, CA
www.toddklick.com

Below are the *Beat by Beat* catch phrases that you can use while: 1) developing your script; 2) working with other writers; 3) preparing index cards; 4) making a pitch; 5) shooting a scene; 6) producing a script; 7) editing a film; 8) acting in a scene.

Aggressor, The — The hero or bad guy shows aggression during Minute 94.

Ally Aid — The ally or love interest takes a positive or significant step toward the hero during Minute 68.

Ally Attack — The bad guy, or secondary bad guy, deeply affects the hero's ally or love interest during Minute 63.

Ally's World — We learn more about the ally and their world during Minute 40.

Another Notch — Minute 4's catch phrase which builds upon the previous minute's The Ratchet. A good phrase to use here is, "If you thought that was bad . . ." as in: "*If you thought that was bad*, now the shark bites the girl and drags her around."

Anxiety Amp — A sought-after truth or object is revealed and causes great anxiety during Minute 32.

At*tension*! — How a movie story starts during Minute 1 of a screenplay. Tension grabs attention.

Bad Guy Threat — The bad guy, or secondary bad guy, threatens hero in some way during Minute 64.

Bad to the Bone — A reference to the George Thorogood song that sums up the bad guy, or secondary bad guy, showing aggression during Minute 71.

Badder to the Bone — A building upon of Minute 71 which is called Bad to the Bone, a reference to the George Thorogood song that sums up the bad guy, or secondary bad guy, showing aggression. Badder to the Bone happens on Minute 72.

Baddest to the Bone — A building upon of Minutes 71 and 72 which are called Bad to the Bone and Badder to the Bone, a reference to the George Thorogood song that sums up the bad guy, or secondary bad guy, showing more aggression. Baddest to the Bone happens on Minute 73.

Bad Guy Boo-Boo — Refers to the bad guy getting hurt during Minute 85. It shows the bad guy is vulnerable and could possibly be defeated.

Bait and Switch — Seems like this new world the hero is experiencing in the movie is positive, but is it really? This happens during Minute 35.

Big Concern, The — The troubled or anxious state of mind, occurring during Minute 16, that happens to either the hero or ally.

Big Quest Prep — Hero prepares for the bigger quest with ally during Minute 28.

Big Quest Prep 2 — Building upon Minute 28's Big Quest Prep, the hero and/or ally's preparation for a bigger quest continues during Minute 29.

Big Unexpected, The — An unexpected moment during Minute 26 that keeps the hero and the audience off balance.

Bleak Meek — Refers to Minute 115 when things look bleak for the meek hero.

Blow, The — The hero or bad guy administers some sort of blow during Minute 103.

Blow-Up, The — Referring to Minute 102 when something blows up either physically or emotionally.

Build, The — Used during Minute 2 where audience anticipation is increased by "building upon" already existing tension. A good phrase to use during this minute is "Not only does" as in: "*Not only does* Casey get a mysterious call from a stranger, but the stranger calls a *third* time."

Cage Slam, The — Refers to Minute 113 when the shark rams his nose into Hooper's cage in *Jaws*.

Captivating Concern —Concern is shown during Minute 69, but with a little more at stake.

Charging Shark — The bad guy takes aggressive action toward the hero and ally during Minute 112.

Damage Done — The bad guy provokes physical or emotional damage during Minute 87.

Danger Watch — A docile hero watches danger approaching during Minute 14.

Dark Twist Chat — The hero talks with a friend, and then there's a dark twist in Minute 56.

Death and Dying — Refers to the prominence of death and dying being the main feature during Minute 96.

Deceit, The — Referring to Minute 105 where some sort of deceit occurs.

Deception, The — Some form of deception, in words or deed, happens during Minute 59.

Deeper Deeper — Referring to Minute 101 where the hero goes deeper into the story.

Difficult Words — A difficult question/request/statement is asked or made during Minute 57.

Discussion, The — Someone important to the hero wants to discuss something significant during Minute 10.

Distress Signal — The hero sees/hears something that distresses him during Minute 31.

Dodge, The — Someone dodges or avoids something during Minute 106.

Double Damage Done — A building upon Minute 87's Damage Done where the bad guy causes *additional* physical or emotional damage during Minute 88.

Engage, The — The hero and/or ally engage the enemy, the enemy intimidates the hero during Minute 51.

Extraordinary, The — Something extraordinary is revealed during Minute 109.

Escort, The — The ally takes, or will take, the hero somewhere during Minute 47.

Final Quest — Depending on how long your story is, somewhere between Minutes 80 and 110 is the last push toward the final battle place.

Flirtin' with Disaster — A reference to the Molly Hatchet song that also refers to movies flirting with some sort of disaster during Minute 62.

Foreboding Fact — The hero is given more knowledge/warning, often ominous, during Minute 49.

Friend Effect — Ally's behavior impacts the hero during Minute 34, either in words or deeds.

Friend or Fist — The hero and ally bond or fight during Minute 6, which defines their relationship and helps us get to know them better.

Friend or Fist 2 — The phrase used to define Minute 7, which builds upon Minute 6's Friend or Fist. During this minute the hero and ally bond or fight, which defines their relationship and helps us get to know them better.

Gap Subtract — Gap between hero and bad guy/ally decreases during Minute 84.

Gets the Better — The bad guy gets the better of hero and/or ally during Minute 114.

Good Does Bad — Someone that seems good does bad during Minute 107.

Gotta Go! — Refers to the hero hurrying off somewhere in Minute 83.

Great Effect, The — Something happens during Minute 21 that greatly impacts the hero.

Harsher Warning — Building upon Minute 11's The Warning, Minute 12 is where a harsher warning or threat is made.

Hero Effect — The hero does something that will immediately or eventually impact the main bad guy during Minute 67.

Hide and Seek — The main object of desire stays hidden during Minute 36.

Hope Might Be Lost — Refers to Minute 118 where it looks like hope might be lost for the hero.

Hugs and Kisses — The hero and ally/love interest show affection during Minute 92.

Hugs and Kisses 2 — Builds upon Minute 92's Hugs and Kisses where the hero and ally/love interest show more affection during Minute 93.

Intimidation, The — The enemy intimidates hero during Minute 53.

Jaw Dropper — A Minute 5 moment that makes the audience's jaw drop. It's where something extraordinary or astonishing happens in a movie.

Kick 'Em While They're Down — The bad guy exerts tremendous effort against hero during Minute 116.

Kiss or Spit — The hero or bad guy shows either aggression or affection during Minute 98.

Kiss or Spit 2 — A building upon Minute 98's Kiss or Spit, where the hero or bad guy shows more aggression or affection during Minute 99.

Kiss or Spit 3 — A building upon Minute 98 and 99's Kiss or Spit, where the hero or bad guy shows even more aggression or affection during Minute 100.

Lightbulb, The — A new positive or negative revelation is made during Minute 54.

Massive Midpoint Moment — A moment between Minutes 55 and 62 when things get way more serious for the hero. It's a radical event that forces the hero into seeing things through to the bitter end.

Mini-Quest, The — During Minute 27, a Mini-Quest happens just before the upcoming Big Quest.

Mystery Mission — Hero and ally interact; there's a mystery that needs to be solved during Minute 78.

Mystery Mission 2 —A building upon Minute 78's Mystery Mission where the hero and ally continue to interact; there's a mystery that needs to be solved during Minute 79.

Need, The — An overriding need, usually expressed by the hero, is shown or expressed during Minute 30.

Needed Knowledge — The ally gives/shows hero needed knowledge during Minute 48.

New Journey — One of the main characters in the movie embarks on a new journey during Minute 70.

New Journey Bond — The hero bonds further with main ally on new journey during Minute 39.

New News — The hero reacts to New News during Minute 44.

Ominous Oh No — The hero sees/does/hears something ominous during Minute 33.

One Bullet Left — Taken from Minute 119 where John McClane in *Die Hard* and Chief Brody in *Jaws* both have only one bullet left when they go to meet the bad guy.

Out of the Ordinary — Hero does something brave and out of the ordinary for him during Minute 45.

Over His Head — The hero or ally realizes he may be in over his head during Minute 37.

Plus Minus — A positive turns into a negative, or a negative turns into a positive during Minute 61.

Portent, The — Something potentially deadly is seen or explained during Minute 50.

Positive Reconnect — The hero reconnects with ally in a positive way during Minute 38.

Positive Step — The hero does something positive toward his goal during Minute 66.

Powder Keg, The — Refers to Minute 120 when the powder keg of a situation either explodes physically or emotionally.

Pursuit, The — The hero discovers something extraordinary or astonishing during Minute 9 that must be pursued.

Push Back — Up until Minute 20 the hero has been pushed around, now it's his turn to push back.

Put into Peril — The hero and/or ally is put into peril during Minute 74.

Ratchet, The — Just like a ratchet wrench escalates the tension in the wrist when tightening a bolt, added tension ratchets the story during Minute 3. A good phrase to use here is "Not only that, but now . . ." as in: "*Not only that, but now* Morpheus tells Trinity they've been compromised — agents are outside!"

Red Alert! — Circumstances grow more serious for hero during Minute 89.

Reprieve — Thing looks really, *really* bleak for hero during Minute 117, but hero does something that might save him.

Rescuing Ally — Refers to Minute 90 when the ally comes to the hero's rescue.

Resistance, The — The hero or ally attacks or resists the bad guy during Minute 65.

Revelation, The — A revelation during Minute 46 that comes in four different forms: 1) Revelations that rock the hero's world; 2) Revelations about the ally; 3) Revelations about the hero; 4) Revelations about the bad guy.

Rumble, The — Refers to Minute 77 where some sort of fight breaks out, either physically or emotionally.

Say Uncle — The common schoolyard phrase that encapsulates what happens during Minute 52. Not only does the enemy intimidate the hero in the previous minute, now he almost defeats him.

Scary Stuff — Hero experiences something scary with ally or love interest during Minute 23.

Scary Stuff 2 — Building upon the previous Minute 23, the hero and/or ally/love interest experience *more* scary stuff during Minute 24.

Scary Stuff 3 — Building upon the previous Minutes 23 and 24, the hero and/or ally/love interest experience *even more* scary stuff during Minute 25.

Sense of Finality — Referring to Minute 108 where either there's a wrap up of the story or a subplot, or there's a sense of impending doom.

Separation, The — The hero and ally separate during Minute 95.

Shocker, The —Something that draws a swift inhalation of breath from the audience that happens to the hero or his allies during Minute 60.

Sideswipe —During Minute 55 there is some kind of surprise — a sideswiping moment — which gives the hero and the audience a jolt.

Skull and Crossbones — Referring to death making an appearance of some sort during Minute 75.

Something Startling Happens — Something startling happens during Minute 8, usually to the hero.

Submission, The — A final warning or threat is made and the hero submits during Minute 13.

Surprised Hero — The bad guy or ally surprises the hero during Minute 81.

Surprise Reveal — During Minute 42 the ally/hero reveals something surprising.

Surprise Reveal 2 — Building upon Minute 42's Surprise Reveal, the ally/hero reveals something even more surprising during Minute 43.

Surprise-Surprise — Refers to the second surprise during Minute 82 that follows Minute 81's Surprised Hero.

Strong Statement — Refers to Minute 110 where a strong statement is made either visually or, most of the time, verbally.

Suffer the Weak — Some sort of suffering or weakness is expressed during Minute 91.

Surprise Reveal — The ally or hero reveals something surprising during Minute 42.

Taping the Knuckles — Refers to Minute 97 where the hero prepares for battle.

Thorny Rose — Things may seem kinda rosy, but there's still ugliness out there during Minute 41.

Threat, The — The bad guy, or secondary bad guys, make a threat or warning during Minute 19.

Tick Tick Boom — Refers to Minute 80, which is just like a stick of dynamite that finally goes off.

Trouble Turn — The event during Minute 18 that will get the hero into trouble later.

Truth Declared — Someone speaks a truth during Minute 22.

Turn for the Worse — Refers to Minute 111 where the story takes a turn for the worse, usually for the hero. A good phrase to use during this minute is "Oh no!' as in: "Darth kills a rebel pilot, and two other rebel ships are shot down. *Oh no!* "

Turning Point — An event that sends the hero, and the story, into a dramatically different direction.

Upper Hand, The — The hero or bad guy gets the upper hand in an aggressive manner during Minute 104.

Valley of Death — A reference to the Old Testament verse, which sums up death making a stronger appearance during Minute 76.

Vital Event — An event during Minute 58 that either alters the hero's life, touches upon the past, reveals the state of a relationship, or poses a threat.

Warning, The — A warning or threat is made during Minute 11.

Whew, That Was Close! — Hero experiences a close call while danger approaches in Minute 15.

World Upside Down — The bad guy turns a good person's world upside down during Minute 17.

Worry Wound — Something worries and wounds our characters during Minute 86.

BEAT BY BEAT TIMELINE

1 Attention!
2 The Build
3 The Ratchet
4 Another Notch
5 Jaw Dropper
6 Friend Or Fist
7 Friend Or Fist 2
8 Something Startling Happens
9 The Pursuit
10 The Discussion
11 The Warning
INCITING INCIDENT (Minute 12)
12 Harsher Warning
13 The Submission
14 Danger Watch
15 Whew, That Was Close!
16 The Big Concern
17 World Upside Down
TURNING POINT 17 (Between 16-18)
18 Trouble Turn
19 The Threat
20 Push Back
21 The Great Effect
22 Truth Declared
23 Scary Stuff
24 Scary Stuff 2
25 Scary Stuff 3
26 The Big Unexpected
27 The Mini-Quest
28 Big Quest Prep
29 Big Quest Prep 2
30 The Need

THE QUEST (Between 29-35)
31 Distress Signal
32 Anxiety Amp
33 Ominous Oh No
34 Friend Effect
35 Bait And Switch
36 Hide And Seek
37 Over His Head
38 Positive Reconnect
39 New Journey Bond
40 Ally's World
41 Thorny Rose
42 Surprise Reveal
43 Surprise Reveal 2
44 New News
45 Out Of The Ordinary
TURNING POINT 45 (Between 44-47)
46 The Revelation
47 The Escort
48 Needed Knowledge
49 Foreboding Fact
50 The Portent
51 The Engage
52 Say Uncle
53 The Intimidation
54 The Lightbulb
55 Sideswipe
56 Dark Twist Chat
57 Difficult Words
58 Vital Event
59 The Deception
60 The Shocker
THE MIDPOINT (Between 55-65)

ACT ONE

Setup

PAGES 1-30

The Main Hero goes about his usual business with his sidekick, oblivious of his flaw. Suddenly an incident occurs that will force him to eventually deal with that flaw. But since he doesn't want to face his flaw, or is in denial about it, he refuses to confront what the incident presented to him. Eventually he . . .

ACT TWO

The Quest's Escalating Complication

PAGES 31-60ish

. . . embarks on a quest that forces him to enter a "dark cave." The Main Hero, with the help of his Sidekick, Maiden, Wise Old Man, and Mother Figure battles the Henchman, Shape-shifter and Villain in this strange dark cave (who all challenge his flaw). Obstacles grow more difficult and complications escalate the deeper the Main Hero goes into the cave. It's at this point the Main Hero either sees a (false) light at the far end of the cave, or the cave collapses in front of him on his way toward the light. This collapse forces the Main Hero to find another way out.

ACT THREE

61 Plus Minus
62 Flirtin' With Disaster
63 Ally Attack
64 Bad Guy Threat
65 The Resistance
66 Positive Step
67 Hero Effect
68 Ally Aid
69 Captivating Concern
70 New Journey
71 Bad To The Bone
72 Badder To The Bone
73 Baddest To The Bone
74 Put Into Peril
75 Skull And Crossbones
TURNING POINT 75 (Between 74-76)
76 Death Tap
77 The Rumble
78 Mystery Mission
79 Mystery Mission 2
80 Tick Tick Boom
81 Surprised Hero
82 Surprise-Surprise
83 Gotta Go!
84 Gap Subtract
85 Bad Guy Boo-Boo

ACT THREE

Death Valley

PAGES 61-85ish

The Main Hero then experiences the darkest moments of his entire life as he continues to fight the Villain who prevents him from exiting the cave. In fact, the Main Hero reaches the lowest point he's ever experienced. Realizing that his only hope of getting out of the cave is to overcome his flaw *and* to face the Villain directly, the Main Hero prepares himself for battle. He then marches toward the Villain for a final, winner-take-all brawl.

ACT FOUR

THE FINAL QUEST (Between 85-100)
86 Worry Wound
87 Damage Done
88 Double Damage Done
89 Red Alert!
90 Rescuing Ally
TURNING POINT 90
91 Suffer The Weak
92 Hugs And Kisses
93 Hugs And Kisses 2
94 The Aggressor
95 The Separation
96 Death And Dying
97 Taping The Knuckles
98 Kiss Or Spit
99 Kiss Or Spit 2
100 Kiss Or Spit 3
101 Deeper Deeper
102 The Blow-Up
103 The Blow
104 The Upper Hand
105 The Deceit
TURNING POINT 105
106 The Dodge
107 Good Does Bad
108 Sense Of Finality
109 The Extraordinary
110 Strong Statement
111 Turn For The Worse
112 Charging Shark
113 The Cage Slam
114 Gets The Better
115 Bleak Meek
116 Kick 'Em While They're Down
117 Reprieve
118 Hope Might Be Lost
119 One Bullet Left
120 Powder Keg

ACT FOUR

Resolution

PAGES 85-120ish

The Main Hero sacrifices his flaw completely on this final quest and suffers great pain because of it, but in doing so he defeats the Villain and finds a way out of the cave. Stepping into the sunlight, the Main Hero is rewarded with a new and better life. (Or, if he doesn't overcome his flaw, he is defeated and we, as an audience, learn from his failure.)

FILMOGRAPHY

The Avengers, 2012, Marvel Studios

A Beautiful Mind, Universal Pictures, DreamWorks Pictures

The Conjuring, 2103, Warner Bros.

Die Hard, 1988, 20th Century Fox

Forrest Gump, 1999, Paramount Pictures

The Godfather, 1972, Paramount Pictures

Gone Girl, 2014, 20th Century Fox

The Hangover, 2009, Warner Bros.

Jaws, 1975, Universal Pictures

Juno, 2007, Fox Searchlight Pictures

Knocked Up, 2007, Universal Pictures

Little Miss Sunshine, 2006, Fox Searchlight Pictures

The Matrix, 1999, Warner Bros. Pictures

Pulp Fiction, 1994, Miramax Films

Raiders of the Lost Ark, 1981, Paramount Pictures

Scream, 1996, Dimension Films

The Sixth Sense, 1999, Hollywood Pictures

Skyfall, 2012, Metro-Goldwyn-Mayer Pictures, Columbia Pictures

Star Wars, 1977, 20th Century Fox

Top Gun, 1988, Paramount Pictures

ABOUT THE AUTHOR

Courtesy of Stephen Paley

Todd Klick is the #1 bestselling author of *Something Startling Happens: The 120 Story Beats Every Writer Needs to Know*; *The Screenwriter's Fairy Tale*; and a contributor to the #1 bestselling Tarcher-Penguin book, *Now Write! Science Fiction, Fantasy and Horror: Speculative Genre Exercises from Today's Best Writers and Teachers*. His stories earned accolades with the prestigious Nicholl Fellowship and the PAGE International screenwriting competitions. Klick has sold and optioned numerous scripts for the stage and screen. He is also a contributor to *The Huffington Post* and *MovieMaker Magazine*. www.toddklick.com.

{ THE MYTH OF MWP }

In a dark time, a light bringer came along, leading the curious and the frustrated to clarity and empowerment. It took the well-guarded secrets out of the hands of the few and made them available to all. It spread a spirit of openness and creative freedom, and built a storehouse of knowledge dedicated to the betterment of the arts.

The essence of the Michael Wiese Productions (MWP) is empowering people who have the burning desire to express themselves creatively. We help them realize their dreams by putting the tools in their hands. We demystify the sometimes secretive worlds of screenwriting, directing, acting, producing, film financing, and other media crafts.

By doing so, we hope to bring forth a realization of 'conscious media' which we define as being positively charged, emphasizing hope and affirming positive values like trust, cooperation, self-empowerment, freedom, and love. Grounded in the deep roots of myth, it aims to be healing both for those who make the art and those who encounter it. It hopes to be transformative for people, opening doors to new possibilities and pulling back veils to reveal hidden worlds.

MWP has built a storehouse of knowledge unequaled in the world, for no other publisher has so many titles on the media arts. Please visit www.mwp.com where you will find many free resources and a 25% discount on our books. Sign up and become part of the wider creative community!

Onward and upward,

Michael Wiese
Publisher/Filmmaker